Code of Professional Ethics of the American Institute for CPCU

Code of Professional Ethics of the American Institute for CPCU

With Commentary by
Eric A. Wiening, CPCU
Assistant Vice President and Ethics Counsel
American Institute for CPCU

Sixth Edition • 1999

American Institute for CPCU
720 Providence Road, Malvern, Pennsylvania 19355-0716

Sixth Edition • Fourth Printing • June 2001

Library of Congress Catalog Number 99-73211
International Standard Book Number 0-89463-089-X

Printed in Canada

Foreword

The American Institute for Chartered Property Casualty Underwriters and the Insurance Institute of America are independent, nonprofit, educational organizations serving the needs of the property and liability insurance business. The Institutes develop a wide range of programs—curricula, study materials, and examinations—in response to the educational requirements of various elements of the business.

The American Institute confers the Chartered Property Casualty Underwriter (CPCU®) professional designation on those who meet the Institute's experience, ethics, and examination requirements.

The Insurance Institute of America offers associate designations and certificate programs in the following technical and managerial disciplines:

Accredited Adviser in Insurance (AAI®)
Associate in Information Technology (AIT)
Associate in Claims (AIC)
Associate in Fidelity and Surety Bonding (AFSB)
Associate in Insurance Accounting and Finance (AIAF)
Associate in Insurance Services (AIS)
Associate in Loss Control Management (ALCM®)
Associate in Management (AIM)
Associate in Marine Insurance Management (AMIM®)
Associate in Personal Insurance (API)
Associate in Premium Auditing (APA®)
Associate in Reinsurance (ARe)
Associate in Research and Planning (ARP®)
Associate in Surplus Lines Insurance (ASLI)
Associate in Underwriting (AU)
Global Environment of Insurance
Insurance Regulation
Program in General Insurance
Program in Supervisory Management
Introduction to Property and Liability Insurance
Introduction to Claims
Introduction to Risk Management

Introduction to Underwriting
Writing at Work
Focus Series

  Topical Presentations—CE Credit

The Center for the Advancement of Risk Management Education (CARME), a division of the American Institute for CPCU and the Insurance Institute of America, serves as the focal point for the Institutes' risk management programs:

  Associate in Risk Management (ARM)
  Risk Management for Public Entities

The Insurance Institute for Applied Ethics was established in 1995 to heighten awareness of the pervasiveness of ethical decision making in insurance and to explore ways to raise the level of ethical behavior among parties to the insurance contract. The Ethics Institute sponsors seminars and workshops on the role of ethics in the insurance transaction. It also identifies and funds practical research projects on ethics-related topics and publishes the findings. In addition, it produces booklets, newsletters, and videotapes on ethics issues.

The Insurance Research Council (IRC) was established in 1977 as an independent, not-for-profit research institute to examine public policy issues that affect property and liability insurers and their customers. In 1998, the IRC was merged into the American Institute for CPCU and became a division of the Institutes. The IRC provides timely and reliable information based on extensive data collection and analyses and conducts empirical studies on a wide range of topics relating to all lines of property and liability insurance. IRC research reports are widely distributed to assist the public and insurers in reaching sound decisions on legislative and regulatory matters. The IRC does not advocate public policy; nor does it directly influence specific legislation or engage in lobbying communications. The IRC is devoted solely to research and the communication of its research findings.

The Institutes began publishing textbooks in 1976 to help students meet the national examination standards. Since that time, we have produced more than ninety individual textbook volumes. Despite the vast differences in the subjects and purposes of these volumes, they all have much in common. First, each book is specifically designed to increase knowledge and develop skills that can improve job performance and help students achieve the educational objectives of the course for which it is assigned. Second, all of the manuscripts of our texts are widely reviewed before publication, by both insurance business practitioners and members of the academic community. All of our texts and course guides also reflect the work of Institute staff members. These writing or editing duties are seen as an integral part of their professional responsibilities, and no staff member earns a royalty based on the sale of our texts. We have proceeded in this way to avoid even the appearance of any conflict of interests. Finally, the revisions of our texts often incorporate improvements suggested by students and course leaders.

We welcome criticisms of and suggestions for improving our publications. It is only with such constructive comments that we can hope to improve the quality of our study materials. Please direct any comments you may have on this text to the Curriculum Department of the Institutes.

Terrie E. Troxel, Ph.D., CPCU, CLU
President and CEO

Preface

This book is intended to serve two primary purposes. First, it is part of the required study material for students preparing to pass examinations leading to the Chartered Property Casualty Underwriter (CPCU®) professional designation. Related material for CPCU students appears in the CPCU 1 Course Guide, which is published by the American Institute for CPCU. Second, this material should be a valuable refresher for CPCUs who wish to review their ethical obligations. In addition to these primary purposes, it is hoped that this book might provide information and inspiration to others with an interest in business ethics, particularly as it applies within insurance, risk management, and related fields.

Ethics has always been part of the CPCU movement. The very first CPCU graduating class in 1943 recited the CPCU Charge:

✳ *In all of my business dealings and activities I agree to abide by the following rules of professional conduct:*

- *I shall strive at all times to ascertain and understand the needs of those whom I serve and act as if their interests were my own; and*

- *I shall do all in my power to maintain and uphold a standard of honor and integrity that will reflect credit on the business in which I am engaged.*

With minor changes, this "Charge," now known as the CPCU Professional Commitment, continues to serve as a pledge that is recited by all CPCUs present at every CPCU conferment ceremony.

For many years, the CPCU Charge provided a succinct ethical standard for CPCUs. A more formal code of ethics was introduced in June of 1976 by the American Institute's Board of Trustees. The original Code of Professional Ethics of the American Institute consisted of four components: a Preamble; Canons, Rules and Guidelines; Disciplinary Rules, Procedures, and Penalties; and Advisory Opinions in the form of Hypothetical Case Studies. With minor changes that were made through the next four editions, these components of the Code have been part of the required CPCU study material since 1978, when the revised, ten-course CPCU program was introduced.

Most components of the Code are included in this book with only minor or editorial changes. Information previously contained in the Preamble of the original Code has instead been incorporated into the Introduction to this book.

As compared with previous editions of the Code, in addition to expanded information in the Introduction, this book adds a Commentary on the Canons, Rules, and Guidelines. It also includes the CPCU Society's Code of Ethics and a Glossary.

Before writing the Commentary and other enhancements for this book, I served for many years as the American Institute staff member responsible for one or more courses in the CPCU curriculum, including the CPCU 1 course, where the Code of Ethics has resided as assigned study material since 1992. My more recent experience includes service as Ethics Counsel for the American Institute. In both roles, I saw a need to provide students with textbook-like material to supplement the bare Code with which students have long struggled. This book addresses that need.

The Commentary on the Canons, Rules, and Guidelines includes all of the Canons, Rules, and Guidelines of the Code, which appear in boldface type in that section of the book. The Canons, Rules, and Guidelines also appear without embellishment in a separate section. These are authoritative statements and should be taken as such. Within the Commentary, the narrative material not in boldface type is added to clarify and support the Code.

Many people contributed to the development of this book. First, I am grateful to James J. Markham, J.D., CPCU, AIC, AIAF, Senior Vice President and General Counsel of the American Institute for CPCU for encouraging me to undertake this project and for reviewing the early manuscripts. I also want to thank the following people who reviewed the manuscript for the Introduction and Commentary and offered some valuable suggestions for improvement:

Blake G. Anderson, CPCU, CLU, AIM
CGL Marketing Department
Kemper Insurance Companies

Norman A. Baglini, Ph.D., CPCU, CLU, AU, ARe
President Emeritus
American Institute for CPCU

Mary Ann Boose, Ph.D., CPCU, CLU
Chairperson and Associate Professor, Department of Insurance and Risk Management
Indiana State University

Lawrence G. Brandon, CPCU, AIM, ARM
Chairman
American Institute for CPCU

Michael S. Cabot, CPCU
President Emeritus
Western Association of Insurance Brokers

John G. DiLiberto, CPCU, CLU, ChFC
President and CEO
National Insurance Crime Bureau

Peter R. Kensicki, DBA, CPCU, CLU, FLMI
Professor/Chairholder of Insurance Studies
Eastern Kentucky University

Richard G. Rudolph, Ph.D., CPCU, ARM, APA, ARP, AIAF, AAM
Principal Consultant
Seaver, Rudolph & Associates

John J. Schiff, Jr., CPCU
Chairman of the Board
Cincinnati Financial Corporation

Michael B. Vehec, CPCU, AIC, AIM, ARP
Vice President, Litigation/Claims Examination
Erie Insurance Group

Bruce D. Williams, CPCU, CLU, ChFC
President/Municipal Services Agency Division
Glatfelter Insurance Group

In closing, I wish to express my appreciation to Dr. Ronald C. Horn, CPCU, CLU, Professor of Insurance Studies (Retired), Baylor University, who, as author and editor of the original Code has contributed far more than any other person to the creation of this text.

Eric A. Wiening

Contents

Introduction

This publication is intended to serve two purposes:

- As part of the required study material for CPCU® candidates, it enables students to meet some of the Educational Objectives articulated in the CPCU 1 Course Guide.
- As a publication that stands on its own, it provides an opportunity for CPCUs who have previously studied the Code to refresh their understanding and appreciation of the Code of Professional Ethics by which the vast majority of CPCUs are bound.

Various statements in this publication assert that "all CPCUs" are bound by the Code. This is a slight oversimplification that avoids wordiness. All who became CPCUs in 1976 or later years are bound by the Code. A relatively small number of CPCUs are not bound by the Code because they both (1) received the CPCU designation before 1976, when the Code was introduced and (2) did not voluntarily agree to be bound by the Code. Soon after the Code's introduction, the great majority of existing CPCUs signed a statement agreeing to be bound by the Code.

Purpose of the Code of Professional Ethics

The Code of Professional Ethics of the American Institute for CPCU (the Code) serves two complementary roles, describing both high aspirational goals and minimum standards of conduct:

1. The high goals described in the Canons challenge all CPCUs and CPCU candidates to aspire to the highest level of ethical performance in all their professional activities.

2. The minimum standards of conduct, described in the Rules, maintain the integrity of the CPCU designation. The public should be able to assume that anybody who is a CPCU meets a certain standard of ethical conduct. All CPCUs are obligated to meet at least the minimum stan-

dards in the Rules, and failure to do so may subject a CPCU—or a CPCU candidate—to disciplinary measures.

The ultimate goal of the Code is to foster highly ethical conduct on the part of all CPCUs. Ethical behavior begins with ethics awareness. The Code is included among CPCU study materials to ensure that all CPCUs understand their ethical obligations. CPCU candidates demonstrate that they have mastered the ethics study materials by passing a CPCU national exam, but ethical behavior involves real-world performance, not merely knowing right answers to exam questions. Without measures to ensure CPCUs' ongoing ethical behavior, the Code would be meaningless. Therefore, the Code includes provisions for its orderly enforcement.

Only the American Institute for Chartered Property Casualty Underwriters is authorized to confer the professional designation Chartered Property Casualty Underwriter (CPCU®). The American Institute confers the CPCU designation only upon individuals who have met the three requirements—education, experience, and ethics—established by the Institute's Board of Trustees.

Having granted the CPCU designation to qualified individuals, the Institute's Board of Trustees also has the authority to take it away or to otherwise discipline CPCUs who violate one or more Rules of the Code. Revoking a person's CPCU designation is the ultimate disciplinary action under the Code; lesser sanctions, such as a reprimand, may also be imposed, depending on the severity of the offense. Some CPCUs who violated one or more Rules of the Code have, indeed, lost the right to remain CPCUs, and others have been reprimanded or otherwise sanctioned.

Requirements for Earning the CPCU Designation

To earn the CPCU designation, candidates must meet education, experience, and ethics requirements. To put the ethics requirement into context, all three of these requirements are explained below.

Education Requirement

Specific details of the American Institute for CPCU's education requirement, which is modified from time to time, are published in the current edition of the AICPCU/IIA Catalog. The education requirement is typically met by passing a national exam in each of nine core courses and also meeting a Related Studies requirement.

- The CPCU curriculum includes nine mandatory courses:
    - CPCU 1 – Ethics, Insurance Perspectives, and Insurance Contract Analysis
    - CPCU 2 – Personal Insurance and Risk Management
    - CPCU 3 – Commercial Property Insurance and Risk Management
    - CPCU 4 – Commercial Liability Insurance and Risk Management
    - CPCU 5 – Insurance Operations
    - CPCU 6 – The Legal Environment of Insurance
    - CPCU 7 – Management
    - CPCU 8 – Accounting and Finance
    - CPCU 9 – Economics
- The Related Studies requirement, sometimes considered an elective, enables CPCU candidates to extend their knowledge of insurance and reinforce their professional competence by allowing them to select a particular field for further study. Courses and programs that meet the Related Studies requirement are specified in the current AICPCU/IIA Catalog and other materials published by the Institute. The most current listing is also available on the Institute's web page at http://www.aicpcu.org.

Since the CPCU program was introduced in 1942, its educational requirement has included not only courses in insurance and risk management but also courses in general business topics that relate to the insurance/risk management environment. This broad education requirement ensures that CPCUs are well-rounded professionals, knowledgeable about not only insurance and risk but also their business environment.

Experience Requirement

CPCU is not the only professional program that includes an experience requirement. Experience requirements give the public "an added assurance of fitness and permanency."[1] The CPCU experience requirement ensures that anyone bearing the CPCU designation has some measure of real-world experience as well as the required book learning.

The American Institute requires each candidate, after registering for his or her last CPCU exam, to complete a form showing that a three-year experience requirement has been met. During the five-year period immediately preceding

---

1. Richard C. Jaffeson, Executive Director, National Certification Commission.

the conferment of the CPCU designation, a candidate must have been en-gaged in acceptable insurance activities for any thirty-six months for a mini-mum of seventeen and a half hours per week. "Insurance experience" is broadly interpreted and includes:

- Insurance sales and related account services
- Insurance activities and services such as claim handling, inspection, loss control, premium auditing, ratemaking, rating, reinsurance, and under-writing
- Support functions such as accounting and bookkeeping, clerical, educa-tion and training, information systems, investment services, legal ser-vices and personnel administration, if performed for a firm or department primarily engaged in insurance
- Job roles such as attorney, certified public accountant, college teacher, consultant, risk manager, or employee of a regulatory authority, salvage company, trade association, trade press, or a similar organization working with or as a part of the insurance industry

A candidate who meets all requirements except the experience requirement becomes a CPCU after he or she has met the experience requirement.

Example

Steve Jones, a college student majoring in insurance, took and passed CPCU 1 through 9 as an undergraduate and also met the Related Studies requirement, but Steve's actual insurance experience is limited to his work as a summer intern for an insurance company. Although he has met the education require-ment and the ethics requirement, Steve will not become a CPCU until he has also met the experience requirement. Assuming they occurred within the five-year period, his internships will count toward the required thirty-six months of experience.

Ethics Requirement

CPCU candidates have always been required to have good moral character. The ethics requirement for CPCU candidates is currently handled as part of the matriculation process. **Matriculation** means the process of enrolling as a student. By matriculating, a CPCU student declares that he or she intends to become a CPCU and agrees to adhere to the Institute's procedures. In signing a matriculation form, candidates also agree to the following statement:

> I agree that as a condition of the acceptance of my application and of my continued good standing as a CPCU candidate and as the holder of the

CPCU designation, I shall abide by the Code of Professional Ethics of the American Institute for Chartered Property Casualty Underwriters.

The matriculation form also requires each applicant to identify two employers or colleagues who will attest that the applicant's conduct remains consistent with the American Institute's Code of Professional Ethics. The Institute may conduct reference checks, both after receiving the matriculation form from the student and again when the student registers for his or her last CPCU exam.

CPCU students are asked to submit the matriculation form with their first CPCU exam registration. Any student who misses this deadline must matriculate as soon as possible. A CPCU student who passes two exams without matriculating will not be permitted to register for a third exam until he or she has successfully matriculated.

Parties Affected by the Code

It is necessary to distinguish among applicants, candidates, designees, and CPCUs, terms that are used throughout this publication.

- An **applicant** is a CPCU student who has submitted a matriculation form that has not yet been approved. In rare cases an applicant is rejected and does not become a candidate.

- A **candidate** is a CPCU student whose matriculation has been approved. No special notice is sent to applicants when their candidacy is approved, as it is in the vast majority of cases. For most purposes, there is no reason why a student should try to classify himself or herself as either a candidate or an applicant. The distinction is important only in an unusual case, when an application is suspended or rejected.

- A **designee** is a person who has earned the CPCU designation, whether or not he or she has officially become a CPCU. Those who have met all requirements but are waiting for the date on which they become CPCUs are referred to as designees; those currently receiving the CPCU designation are also considered designees.

  CPCUs commonly use additional jargon: Those who have just received the CPCU designation are commonly called **new designees**, and they may be referred to as new designees for their first year, until another group of graduates become new designees.

- A **CPCU** is a person currently holding the CPCU designation. If someone's designation is revoked or suspended, that person is no longer a CPCU and is no longer permitted to use the CPCU designation.

Applicants

By submitting a matriculation form along with the matriculation fee, a person may matriculate as a CPCU candidate at any time, even without registering for a CPCU exam. Technically, CPCU students who have not matriculated are not yet bound by the Code of Professional Ethics. As a practical matter, every student becomes subject to the Code long before completing CPCU studies, since students are barred from taking a third CPCU exam unless they have matriculated.

Questions on the matriculation form, along with a reference check, are used to identify applicants whose eligibility as a CPCU candidate should be questioned for ethics reasons. Although the ethics requirement is taken seriously, an applicant should not be unduly concerned that his or her matriculation will be rejected because of some incident in the past. To resolve any concerns, applicants who are concerned about their eligibility to become candidates should matriculate as soon as possible.

In serious cases, a student's matriculation application may be rejected. In others, an applicant's eligibility to become a candidate and take further CPCU exams may be suspended for a period of time—or indefinitely.

CPCU Candidates

All CPCU candidates become subject to the binding effect of the Code when they matriculate with the American Institute, and they are bound as long as they remain candidates. Since there is no term limit on CPCU candidacy, a matriculated CPCU student remains a candidate until conferment of the designation, unless the candidate's conferment has been deferred or the candidacy has been suspended or revoked.

CPCUs

The Code of Professional Ethics was introduced in 1976, and every CPCU whose designation was conferred in 1976 or later is bound by the Code. In addition, CPCUs who had previously received their designation were strongly urged to file a written election with the American Institute, as an act of good faith and in the public interest, to be bound by the Code, in order that all objectives of the Code might be achieved. Most of these "older" CPCUs voluntarily agreed to be bound by the Code.

In short, the Code applies to the overwhelming majority of CPCUs, including everyone who became a CPCU during the past twenty-some years. However, a few CPCUs who received their designations before 1976 are not bound by the Code and are not subject to discipline or penalties under the Code. If the

Institute's Ethics Counsel receives a complaint directed against a CPCU not bound by the Code, the case must be dismissed for lack of jurisdiction.

The strongest sanction available to the American Institute for CPCU is the right to revoke a CPCU's designation. Upon losing the CPCU designation, a person also loses the right to retain membership in the CPCU Society, which is a membership organization open only to holders of the CPCU designation. As a membership organization independent of the American Institute, the CPCU Society has its own separate Code of Ethics and the right to suspend or revoke a person's Society membership even if a person retains the CPCU designation. An excerpt from the CPCU Society's Code of Ethics appears elsewhere in this publication. In at least one case in which the American Institute had no jurisdiction over a pre-1976 CPCU, the CPCU Society has expelled a member on the basis of that CPCU's unethical conduct.

Components of the Code

This commentary primarily examines the Canons, Rules, and Guidelines of the Code of Professional Ethics. The Code includes Disciplinary Rules, Procedures, and Penalties, which appear later in this publication and detail the specific process by which the Code is administered and enforced. Hypothetical Case Studies, a third component of the Code, are also included in this publication.

From time to time the American Institute also publishes formal Advisory Opinions. Some Advisory Opinions are discussed in this publication in connection with the Canons and Rules to which they relate. The Institute may also publish additional Advisory Opinions, and it publishes study materials such as the CPCU 1 Course Guide and other materials designed to assist CPCUs and CPCU candidates in interpreting the various Code provisions, understanding their rationale, and applying them to frequently encountered situations that require ethical judgments.

Canons, Rules, and Guidelines

The Canons, Rules, and Guidelines of the Code are discussed in the next section of this publication, and they are also reproduced without commentary in a separate section. The Canons, Rules, and Guidelines serve distinct functions:

- The **Canons** are broad aspirational concepts.
- The **Rules** are specific, enforceable standards that prescribe the minimum levels of required professional conduct. They are enforceable because sanctions may be imposed upon any CPCU or candidate found guilty of a Rule violation.

- The **Guidelines** are provided to help candidates and CPCUs interpret other Code provisions, especially the Rules. Guidelines are directly enforceable only where they are specifically mentioned in a Rule and therefore become part of that Rule. As detailed later, the enforceable Guidelines refer to the use of the CPCU designation and the CPCU key—for example, they explain when it is appropriate to use the letters "CPCU" and where it is appropriate to display the CPCU key.

The nine Canons in the Code are general standards of an aspirational and inspirational nature, lofty goals reflecting the fundamental spirit of altruism that all true professionals share. They are maxims that on their merits serve as model standards of exemplary professional conduct. The Canons also express the general concepts and principles from which the more specific Rules are derived.

Each of the Canons in the Code is followed by one or more related Rules. Unlike the Canons, the Rules are specific mandatory and enforceable standards. The Rules prescribe the absolute minimum level of ethical conduct required of every CPCU, regardless of occupational position. Any individual subject to the Code who violates a Rule faces the possibility of disciplinary action. Only the Rules are enforceable. In the absence of a Rule violation, violations of Canons and/or Guidelines will not constitute sufficient grounds for disciplinary action.

After the Rules that follow each Canon are related Guidelines. Guidelines assist CPCUs and CPCU candidates in interpreting the various Code provisions, understanding their rationale, and applying them to frequently encountered situations that require ethical judgment. Individuals subject to the Code will be exposed to the possibility of disciplinary action for violations of any Guidelines that have been incorporated by reference into the Rules.

Hypothetical Case Studies (HCSs)

When the Code was introduced, it obviously had no case history. There had been no complaints or disciplinary cases to which it had been applied. To illustrate how the Code would be applied, a series of advisory opinions in the form of "Hypothetical Case Studies" accompanied the first edition of the published Code. These cases continue to appear in this edition of the Code, with minor updates or revisions that have become necessary over time.

The HCSs do not involve actual situations. They efficiently pose a wide variety of ethical questions and issues to which the Code might be applied. They also provide some insights as to how the drafters of the Code expected that it would be applied. Following the discussion of each Canon, this commentary lists the HCSs that apply the Canon and its related Rules.

Advisory Opinions

Whenever substantial questions of interpretation arise, CPCUs and CPCU candidates are strongly encouraged to request **Advisory Opinions** from the American Institute. Only the **Board of Ethical Inquiry (BEI)** is authorized to issue Advisory Opinions on behalf of the American Institute. Requests may be directed to the Institute's **Ethics Counsel**, who chairs the BEI.

Advisory opinions may take two forms—unpublished and published.

- **Unpublished advisory opinions** are informal and intended solely for the guidance of the individuals to whom they are issued.
- **Published advisory opinions** are formal, intended for the guidance of all persons subject to the Code.

Unpublished opinions may lead to a published opinion. For example, as use of the Internet evolved, the Institute's Ethics Counsel received several requests for guidance on the appropriate use of the CPCU key and designation on Web pages. Naturally, these questions had not been contemplated when the Code was drafted in the 1970s. Informal, unpublished advisory opinions were provided in response to specific questions. However, it seemed wise to issue a formal opinion that would serve as a consistent guide for all CPCUs. After discussion, the Board of Ethical Inquiry unanimously approved an Advisory Opinion that was published in the *CPCU Journal* in late 1998; this Advisory Opinion appears in this publication in the discussion of Canon 8.

Disciplinary Rules, Procedures, and Penalties

The right to use the CPCU designation is a privilege granted by the Board of Trustees and conditioned upon full compliance with the *Rules of Professional Conduct*. The Board of Trustees reserves the power to suspend or revoke the privilege or approve other penalties recommended by the Board of Ethical Inquiry, the body charged with the responsibility of investigating and adjudicating alleged Rule violations. Disciplinary penalties are imposed as warranted by the severity of the offense and its attendant circumstances. All disciplinary actions are undertaken in accordance with published procedures and penalties designed to ensure the proper enforcement of the Rules within the framework of due process and equal protection of the laws.

The *Disciplinary Rules, Procedures, and Penalties*, which appear in their entirety elsewhere in this publication, provide a fairly detailed description of the procedures to be followed when a CPCU or candidate might have violated one or more Rules of the Code, and they also describe the sanctions that may be imposed.

Procedures

It is important that procedural information be available *as a reference* to CPCUs or candidates who become subject to discipline under the Code. The procedural information is also relevant to CPCUs and others who might want to bring a formal complaint under the Code. And, of course, it is relevant to those who enforce the Code.

Although this information must be available to those who need it, there would be little point in focusing this commentary on the procedures rather than the desired behavior. This point is illustrated by an anecdote.

> It is a basic principle of testing that an exam should identify people who can exhibit the desired skills. A test to evaluate military personnel for promotion should therefore identify those who have the best chance of performing well at a higher rank. But for some questions on one test, it was discovered that the people most likely to provide the right answers were the ones with an unfavorable military record. It turned out that these questions were the ones dealing with penalties for misbehavior. The ones who had experienced these penalties knew the rules very well. The ones whose behavior had been above reproach did not need to know the penalty procedures that were followed in disciplining those who broke the rules.

The point is that most CPCUs should have little need to know the procedures that would be invoked if their ethics are questioned. It is more productive to study the characteristics of ethical behavior than to study in detail the penalties for unethical behavior.

Brief Summary of the Disciplinary Process

All complaints alleging violation of the Code of Professional Ethics should be submitted in writing to the American Institute's Ethics Counsel.[2] If the American Institute has jurisdiction and the claim has sufficient merit, a formal investigation is begun and a copy of the complaint is provided to the person or persons against whom the complaint is lodged, who is given an opportunity to respond.

The specific nature of any investigation depends on the circumstances of the complaint. Ultimately, a three-member Hearing Panel of the Board of Ethical Inquiry (BEI) makes a recommendation to the entire BEI. The BEI recommendation, in turn, is considered by the Ethics Policy Committee of the American Institute's Board of Trustees. All revocations and suspensions of the privilege to use the CPCU designation are reported in writing to the American Institute's Board of Trustees.

---

2. The address is: Ethics Counsel, American Institute for CPCU, 720 Providence Road, PO Box 3016, Malvern, PA 19355-0716, USA.

Parties bringing a complaint are sometimes frustrated by the amount of time involved in resolving it. However, the lengthy detailed process described in the *Disciplinary Rules, Procedures, and Penalties* ensures a high degree of fairness to persons who are the subject of a complaint.

As discussed in detail in connection with Canon 3, some Rules violations involving criminal conviction may subject a CPCU or candidate to automatic suspension without the procedural steps that might otherwise be involved. The conviction itself serves as objective evidence that a Rule has been violated.

The preceding information is an incomplete summary. Readers desiring more detail about the disciplinary process are urged to examine the complete *Disciplinary Rules, Procedures, and Penalties*.

Sanctions and Penalties Under the Code

The sanctions that might be applied to CPCU applicants and candidates differ somewhat from those applicable to CPCUs.

CPCU Applicants and Candidates

Applicant cases typically involve past activities of a questionable nature that fall under the Rules of Canons 3 and 4. Most candidate cases involve cheating on a CPCU exam, a violation of the Rules under Canon 3.

Both applicants and candidates may be penalized by being denied admission to further CPCU exams, either indefinitely or for a specified period of time. The BEI may also withhold awarding the CPCU designation, pending receipt of convincing proof of the candidate's full and complete rehabilitation. Candidates may also be subject to admonition, reprimand, or censure, depending on the nature and severity of the offense.

Automatic Suspension of Candidacy   According to the Code as revised in 1995, a CPCU candidate is immediately suspended from further participation in the CPCU program if the candidate is convicted—by verdict, guilty plea, or plea of nolo contendere—of any crime that violates the Rules of Professional Conduct. This suspension will last indefinitely, or until the BEI has been convinced that that person is again fit to use the designation.

Only certain crimes violate the Rules of Professional Conduct. The distinctions are discussed later in connection with Rule R3.3.

CPCUs

The BEI may impose any of five sanctions upon a CPCU who is subject to the Code and found guilty of a Rules violation:

1. Private admonition, including a request to cease and desist

2. Reprimand (informal rebuke given limited publication)

3. Censure (formal rebuke given wide publication)

4. Suspension of the privilege to use the designation, indefinitely or for a specific time period

5. Revocation of the designation

The terms "limited publication" and "wide publication" are not defined in the Code, and the nature of the publication is decided on a case-by-case basis. If a case is not serious, it might be that only the parties to the complaint are informed of the decision. In other, more serious cases, the action is published in the *CPCU News*, a periodical sent to all current members of the CPCU Society. The CPCU is named, but the nature of the charge might not be described in the publication.

There is a fine line between suspension and revocation. Suspension is a slightly less severe sanction that implies the possibility that the designee might at some future time be permitted to use the CPCU designation. A CPCU whose designation has been revoked may also apply for reinstatement. In one recent case, a CPCU's right to use the designation was reinstated following a period of revocation.

Automatic Suspension of CPCU Designation   In most circumstances, a CPCU may be disciplined only after an investigation leading to a vote by the BEI. However, according to the fifth edition of the Code, as revised in 1995, a CPCU's designation is immediately suspended if the CPCU is convicted, by verdict, guilty plea, or plea of nolo contendere, of any crime that violates the Rules of Professional Conduct. This suspension will last indefinitely, or until the BEI has been convinced that that party is again fit to use the designation.

The preceding information is an incomplete summary. Readers desiring more detail are urged to examine the complete *Disciplinary Rules, Procedures, and Penalties* appearing elsewhere in this publication.

Support for the Code of Professional Ethics

Both the American Institute for CPCU and the CPCU Society actively promote ethical behavior, not only among CPCUs but also in the broader insurance and risk management community, as illustrated by several examples:

- Ethics Awareness Month, occurring each March, was established in 1990 by the American Institute for CPCU, the CPCU Society, The American College, and the Society of Financial Service Professionals (formerly the American Society of CLU & ChFC). Ethics Awareness Month is designed to promote awareness of ethical issues affecting the insurance and financial services industries. More than 270 companies and associations and nearly 400 CPCU and CLU chapters nationwide participate in this annual event.

- The Insurance Institute for Applied Ethics, founded in 1995 by the American Institute for CPCU, promotes research and ethics awareness in insurance.
- The CPCU Society encourages professionalism, continuing education, and high ethical standards in the insurance industry. The CPCU Society also publishes and enforces its own Code of Ethics.

Commentary on the Canons, Rules, and Guidelines of the Code of Professional Ethics

The Canons, Rules, and Guidelines of the Code of Professional Ethics of the American Institute for CPCU (the Code) are examined in this section, along with relevant published Advisory Opinions. The official wording of the Code appears in boldface type, accompanied by discussion and examples. The bold-faced portions of this reading are formal position statements, while other portions are informal commentary, designed to help CPCU candidates and CPCUs understand the official provisions of the Code by which they are bound.

The complete text of the Canons, Rules, and Guidelines, without commentary, appears elsewhere in this publication.

Canon 1 – Altruism

CPCUs should endeavor at all times to place the public interest above their own.

The public interest comes first, before personal interests. The essence of this Canon is captured in one word: altruism. The word "altruism" is not often used in everyday speech. But it will often be used in our discussion of ethics.

Altruism

(1) Unselfish concern for the welfare of others; selflessness. (2) In ethics, the doctrine that the general welfare of society is the proper goal of an individual's actions: opposed to egoism.[3]

It is no accident that the very first words of the Code deal with altruism. The most fundamental objective of the Code is to serve the public interest. Other Canons, along with the Rules and Guidelines, clarify "the public interest" and how CPCUs are to go about endeavoring to put it first.

Canon 1 states a lofty goal, one that cannot humanly be attained "at all times." But that does not make the goal faulty. A CPCU who seriously attempts to always put others first will succeed more often than a person who does not pursue such a goal.

Rule R1.1 – Duty to Understand and Abide by All Rules

A CPCU has a duty to understand and abide by all *Rules* of conduct which are prescribed in the Code of Professional Ethics of the American Institute.

The Canons of the Code set high goals—goals to aspire to even though they will not always be reached, targets to aim for even though they will not always be hit. The Rules, on the other hand, specify minimum standards of behavior that *must* be maintained. Violation of Rule R1.1 or any other Rule can lead to sanctions against a CPCU or candidate.

At first glance, Rule R1.1 seems unnecessary and redundant.

- This Rule seems unnecessary because it should go *without saying* that CPCUs need to understand the Rules by which they have agreed to be bound. Moreover, it seems highly unlikely that a CPCU would be formally charged with a Code violation solely because he or she does not

---

3. *Webster's New World Dictionary Third College Edition, s.v.* "altruism."

understand the Rules. CPCU candidates who do not understand the Rules might not pass the CPCU 1 exam, but that's another matter.

- This Rule seems redundant because failure to abide by any other Rule would provide grounds for a sanction under the Code.

So what roles does Rule R1.1 serve? First, R1.1 serves to introduce the other Rules by making it clear that CPCUs are obligated to understand and abide by them. Second, R1.1 eliminates the possibility that a CPCU, charged with violation of another Rule, could use ignorance as a defense.

It is said that ignorance of the law is no excuse. Likewise, ignorance of the Rules of the Code is no excuse. A CPCU or candidate who does not remain aware of the Rules by which he or she is bound is not excused from abiding by them. Any CPCU who claims he or she cannot be charged with a Rules violation because he or she did not understand the Rules literally admits that he or she has violated Rule R1.1.

Example

John Doe, a CPCU for ten years, puts an enlarged CPCU key on his new business stationery in violation of Rule R8.1 (discussed later). It had been many years since John studied the Code, and he had forgotten that the Code specifies the ways in which the key may be used.

Was a Rule violated? Though he had good intentions, John still violated Rule R8.1 of the Code. Because he was unaware of Rule R8.1, he has also violated Rule R1.1.

What should John do? Obviously, John should have remained aware of the Code he studied as a CPCU candidate. Once he becomes aware of the violation, John should discontinue his use of the inappropriate stationery. It would be a good idea for John to also review the entire Code.

Rule R1.2 – Actions by Others

A CPCU shall not advocate, sanction, participate in, cause to be accomplished, otherwise carry out through another, or condone any act which the CPCU is prohibited from performing by the Rules of this Code.

The Rules of Professional Conduct apply not only to actions of a CPCU, but also to actions of others when Rule R1.2 is violated. Naturally, CPCUs should not act through others to accomplish things they cannot ethically do on their own. Any CPCU who does so is as guilty as if he or she had personally committed the unethical act.

But R1.2 goes further. CPCUs also should not "sanction" or "condone" actions that would be unethical if committed by the CPCU. People who work in insurance, risk management, and related fields often become aware of another party's unethical conduct. The question is, what must a CPCU do when faced with unethical acts initiated by others?

A CPCU violates the Code if he or she sanctions or condones actions by others that are contrary to the Rules of the Code. At minimum, a CPCU should not indicate approval of unethical activities. Rather than actively or passively approving unethical behavior, a CPCU should endeavor to support the public interest by encouraging behavior that meets ethical standards.

Guidelines

The Guidelines are not binding. That is, CPCUs and candidates cannot be sanctioned for failure to meet the standards mentioned in the Guidelines (with one exception noted later). However, the Guidelines are extremely useful in interpreting the Rules and clarifying the aspirational goals of the Canons.

Guideline G1.1 – The Public Interest

By stipulating at the outset that "CPCUs Should Endeavor at All Times to Place the Public Interest Above Their Own," *Canon 1* serves as the fundamental goal of the entire *Code of Professional Ethics*. The other *Code* Standards are essentially attempts to define the "public interest" (and hence the ethical obligations of CPCUs) in more specific terms. Accordingly, the format of the *Code* is best understood by reading *Canon 1*, asking the question, "how?" and then reading the first two Rules. That is to say, how do CPCUs go about endeavoring at all times to place the public interest above their own? Answer: at a *minimum*, by understanding and obeying all the *Rules* in the Code (as specified in *R1.1* and *R1.2*) and then, beyond the expected minimums, by *striving* to meet the more lofty standards expressed in the *Canons* and the *Guidelines*.

The aspirational goal of *Canon 1* is more easily expressed than achieved. Indeed, one doubts whether any profession can ultimately make good the claim that all of its practitioners are forever guided by an attitude of altruism and a spirit of unselfish devotion to the needs of others. Nonetheless, a formal commitment to altruism is probably the single most important characteristic which distinguishes professional from unprofessional behavior.

This Guideline restates the points made earlier in our discussion. It is not easy to consistently place the public interest above one's own. However, it is still a lofty goal toward which all CPCUs should strive.

Guideline G1.2 – Conflicts of Interest

In the performance of his or her professional services, a CPCU should avoid even the appearance of impropriety and should generally act each day in a manner that will best serve the CPCU's own professional interests in the long run. This *Guideline*, when taken along with the other provisions of the *Code*, should pose no insurmountable problems of priority in the context of most everyday situations, since the best long-term professional interests of a CPCU ordinarily do not conflict either with the public interest or with other specific interests. However, it should be acknowledged that potential conflicts of interest may arise, or may appear to arise, because many CPCUs simultaneously serve two or more "masters," and they must somehow balance the various interests with their own personal interests and the best interests of the general public. For example, a CPCU who is employed by an insurance company may serve his or her immediate superior, the corporation, the stockholders, the policyholders, agents, and industry associations. An agent may serve his or her clients, two or more insurers, and his or her business partners, stockholders, or associates.

Strict compliance with all the *Rules* of this *Code*, including R1.2, should enable a CPCU to resolve such potential conflicts of interest which may arise. However, when there is good reason for a person subject to the *Code* to be uncertain as to the ethical propriety of a specific activity or type of conduct, that person should refrain from engaging in such activity or conduct until the matter has been clarified. Any CPCU or CPCU candidate who needs assistance in interpreting the *Code* is encouraged to request an advisory opinion from the American Institute's Board of Ethical Inquiry.

The highest standards of professional conduct require more than avoiding improper behavior. G1.2 suggests avoiding even the appearance of impropriety. At the same time, G1.2 points out that the job roles of many CPCUs appear to present a built-in conflict of interests. Many CPCUs have jobs that require them to serve two masters simultaneously.

Insurance and risk management professionals are not alone in having a conflict of interest. The same challenge affects other professionals. Physicians are increasingly challenged to provide appropriate health care services to their patients while serving the administrative requirements of managed care organizations. Accountants who are hired to examine an organization's financial records according to generally accepted accounting principles might uncover issues that reflect poorly on the organization that pays them but must nonetheless be included in the accountant's report.

How can a CPCU avoid ethical impropriety in the face of conflicting priorities? G1.2 suggests first that one should act in the manner that will best serve the CPCU's professional interests in the long run. Another good piece of advice is to do everything possible to avoid even the appearance of impropriety.

When a certain type of activity might be considered unethical, G1.2 advises that one refrain from the activity until the matter has been clarified. One may also request the Board of Ethical Inquiry to provide assistance in interpreting the Code. Such requests should be directed to the Ethics Counsel at the American Institute for CPCU. The resulting clarification will usually take the form of an informal advisory opinion.

Example

Molly Wood, CPCU, serves as the treasurer of a civic organization that purchases its insurance from Molly's employer, ABC Insurance Company. Molly recently discovered an error in the civic organization's insurance policy and asked the organization's insurance agent to have the policy revised. A month later, the agent had not returned a revised policy, so Molly accessed the company records and made the change herself.

For the sake of discussion, let's assume that everybody would agree that the policy contained an error and all Molly did was correct it. Has she done anything wrong? She found a straightforward way to accomplish what needed to be done, and she did it. But Molly was in a unique situation in representing both the insurer and the insured. Most insureds have no right to access the insurer's computer system and make changes in their own policies. Acting as an insured, Molly likewise had no right to change the insurance company's records. Even if no harm was done, there is an appearance of impropriety in this situation that would best have been avoided.

Was a Rule violated? The only Rule that appears to come even close is R4.1, examined later, and even then the situation would probably best be resolved between Molly and her employer.

What should she have done? The procedures Molly should have followed could differ, depending on Molly's responsibilities with the civic organization, any applicable premium adjustments, her relationship with the insurance agent, and her job with the insurance company. It would appear that she could have avoided any conflict by acting like any other insured whose dealings would take place through the insurance agent. G1.2 also suggests refraining from a questionable activity until the matter has been clarified. If direct action were somehow necessary, it would be wise for Molly to involve her supervisor or some other employee who has no interest in the civic organization and, consequently, no potential for a conflict of interest. As a further source of clarification, Molly could have obtained advice in interpreting the Code from the American Institute.

Guideline G1.3 – Applicable to All CPCUs (and Candidates)

The ethical obligation to place the public interest above personal interests or financial gain extends to every CPCU, regardless of whether or not the CPCU's occupational position requires direct contact with actual or prospective insurance consumers.

When discussing ethics and insurance, it is easy to focus on producers, claims representatives, and others who have direct customer contact that creates the most obvious opportunities for a conflict of interests. This Guideline serves as a reminder that CPCUs in almost every function can face situations in which they are tempted to place their own interests, or other interests, above the interest of the public.

Guideline G1.4 – Preferential Treatment

Nothing in these *Guidelines* should be interpreted to mean that insurance purchasers should be given priority over deserving insurance claimants since the needs and best interests of insurance purchasers are in fact served only when all deserving insurance claimants, including third-party liability claimants, are accorded prompt, equitable, and otherwise fair treatment.

Placing the public interest above one's own might suggest that CPCUs ought to bend over backwards to provide benefits to which some people are not entitled. This Guideline makes it clear that that is not the intent, and that the public interest is best served when all parties receive fair treatment.

Other Related Code Provisions

As this reading progresses, it will become obvious that many of the provisions in the Code are closely linked with other provisions. This is especially true with Canon 1, since altruism is the foundation of the entire Code. Also, because they mention the other Rules, both R1.1 and R1.2 are inevitably linked to every other Rule of the Code.

Relevant Hypothetical Case Studies

Hypothetical Case Studies (HCSs) appear elsewhere in this publication. The Hypothetical Case Studies illustrate ways in which the Code's drafters expected it to be applied in case situations. The HCSs also help to demonstrate the interrelationships among various provisions in the Code. The following

Hypothetical Case Studies deal in some manner with Canon 1 and its related provisions:

- HCS 102
- HCS 103
- HCS 105
- HCS 114
- HCS 119

Review Questions

Suggested answers appear elsewhere in this publication.

1. What is altruism?
2. Why is altruism the one characteristic that most distinguishes professional behavior from unprofessional behavior?
3. How should CPCUs go about placing the public interest above their own?

Canon 2 – Continuing Professional Development

CPCUs should seek continually to maintain and improve their professional knowledge, skills, and competence.

This is the only Canon that has just one Rule. While the Canon sets a high goal that includes *improving* professional knowledge, skills, and competence, Rule R2.1 makes it clear that each CPCU *must* at least *maintain* competence in his or her area of practice.

Rule R2.1 – Maintaining Professional Competence

A CPCU shall keep informed on those technical matters that are essential to the maintenance of the CPCU's professional competence in insurance, risk management, or related fields.

CPCUs are by definition an educated group. Nobody becomes a CPCU without passing at least ten national exams. Canon 2 emphasizes the point that professionals never stop learning. CPCUs should continually try to serve the public interest by improving their abilities through a combination of education and experience. More competence is always better.

The CPCU curriculum includes a wide array of topics dealing with all lines of insurance as well as insurance operations, law, management, accounting, finance, and economics. After studying all of these subjects, should a CPCU also be required to maintain and improve his or her knowledge in all of these areas? That would not be realistic. CPCUs are expected to serve the public interest as practicing professionals, not as professional students. CPCUs are required to keep informed on the matters that are essential to their competent performance as insurance or risk management professionals—or, if applicable, in the related field in which they practice.

The implications of CPCUs' competence extend beyond service to their customers, colleagues, and professional contacts. The competence of every practicing CPCU reflects on the image and reputation of every other CPCU. Other issues relating to maintaining the integrity of the CPCU designation are discussed in connection with Canon 8.

Guidelines

The Guidelines elaborate on the points expressed above.

Guideline G2.1 – Ethical Obligation for Continuous Learning

Though knowledge and skills alone do not ensure that an individual will adhere to high ethical standards, knowledge and skills are requisites to the high levels of competence and performance rightfully expected of all professionals. Indeed, to the extent that an individual purports to be a professional and yet does not maintain high levels of competence and performance, that individual engages in unethical conduct which is in the nature of a misrepresentation.

In order to earn the CPCU designation, every CPCU candidate demonstrated a mastery of insurance and related subjects by successfully completing a series of rigorous qualifying examinations of the American Institute for Chartered Property Casualty Underwriters. However, for any individual to maintain and improve the knowledge and skills which are requisites to high levels of competence and performance, it is essential for that individual to continue studying throughout his or her working life. This is especially true for practitioners in a business like insurance, which is characterized not only by its existing complexities but also by rapid changes in the business and in the legal, economic, and social environments within which it operates.

In recognition of the foregoing, each and every CPCU has an *ethical* obligation to engage actively and continuously in appropriate educational activities.

This Guideline makes it clear that continuously improving performance is more than a good thing to practice. The Guideline is much stronger than that. CPCUs have an *ethical* obligation of continuous learning.

Guideline G2.2 – A Matter of Individual Judgment

At a *minimum*, as specified in Rule R2.1, "A CPCU shall keep informed on those technical matters that are essential to the maintenance of the CPCU's professional competence in insurance, risk management, or related fields." Since CPCUs serve as agents, brokers, underwriters, claims representatives, actuaries, risk managers, regulators, company executives and specialists in a wide variety of insurance-related fields, the *Rule* does not attempt to prescribe the specific technical matters that are essential to the maintenance of professional competence in each of the numerous specialties. Instead, it is left to the judgment of each CPCU to decide, in the light of his or her occupational position, the content and form of continuing education that will satisfy the ethical obligation under R2.1.

It would not be appropriate to develop a single set of standards that apply to the vast array of occupations in which CPCUs are engaged. Each CPCU may apply professional judgment to determine how best to meet his or her ethical obligations that satisfy R2.1 and aspire to the goals of Canon 2.

Example

Don Clark, CLU, CPCU, acquired his CPCU designation in 1980, when he was selling both life insurance and personal lines property and liability insurance. Since 1990 he has concentrated exclusively on life insurance and financial planning, and he regularly reads periodicals and attends seminars to keep up with this rapidly changing specialty. However, he has not met the state continuing education requirements to maintain his license to sell property/liability insurance, so the license has lapsed. He continues to use the CPCU designation after his name on business cards and stationery, and his signature block in all business correspondence reads "Don Clark, CLU, CPCU."

Was a Rule violated? Don has done exactly what Rule R2.1 requires, and it appears that his activities are also consistent with the lofty goals of Canon 2. Under specific situations that have not been presented, it is possible that Don's use of the designation would violate Rule R6.3, discussed later.

Some readers might wonder whether Don has inappropriately positioned the CPCU designation after his name. The Code of Professional Ethics contains no Rule regarding the sequence in which a CPCU should list his or her designations. Most CPCUs with more than one designation list CPCU first because they consider it the most substantial and important. As a life insurance specialist, Don apparently believes that CLU (Chartered Life Underwriter) is the most relevant designation he holds.

What Should Don Do? Even though he is a CPCU, Don might reconsider whether he should routinely continue to hold out his CPCU designation as a professional credential. The CPCU designation implies expertise in property and liability insurance, and Don's personal expertise is apparently out of date. In any case, Don should also pay close attention to Rule R6.3 and not misrepresent or conceal his current limitations. If Don should reenter the property-liability field, he should be sure to bring his expertise back up to speed in any area in which he practices.

Guideline G2.3 – No Mandatory Recertification

A number of other professions have established mandatory continuing education requirements, under the terms of which a member usually faces severe penalties unless he or she periodically certifies that at least one of the specified continuing education options has been met. At present and for the foreseeable future, the Trustees of the American Institute have no plans to require CPCUs to certify periodically that they have met the obligations under *Rule R2.1*. However, because the maintenance of professional competence is considered a minimum obligation of every CPCU, it has been given the status of a *Rule* under the *Code*. The Board of Ethical Inquiry will investigate alleged violations of *Rule R2.1,* and it may impose upon violators such penalties as are warranted. Furthermore, if a CPCU is accused of violating any other *Rule* in the *Code,* the Board may, at its discretion, require the accused to furnish evidence of compliance with *Rule R2.1.*

Rule R2.1 makes it very clear that CPCUs have an ethical obligation to continuous learning, and any CPCU who fails to comply with a Rule of the Code can be sanctioned by the Board of Ethical Inquiry. Since R2.1 requires CPCUs to keep informed, it would appear that CPCUs could be sanctioned for failure to meet a continuing education standard. For reasons discussed here and earlier, the Institute does not require CPCUs to comply with a point-counting type of "continuing education" standard. Therefore, it is unlikely that a CPCU would be sanctioned *solely* for failure to keep informed. If a CPCU's performance is so inadequate that it leads to an ethics complaint, R2.1 might be one of several rules considered by the Board in determining appropriate action.

Example

The president of the Valley CPCU Chapter wrote the Board of Ethical Inquiry to complain that Rose Blume, CPCU, occasionally attends chapter meetings where she socializes with other members, but she has never participated in any of the educational seminars or workshops sponsored by the chapter. A long-time surplus lines underwriter, Rose is not licensed and therefore is not required to meet any continuing education requirements. When contacted by the chapter's president, Rose reportedly stated that she passed the exams to earn her CPCU and that's enough.

Was a Rule violated? Rule R2.1 does not require Rose, or any other CPCU, to participate in CPCU seminars or workshops, nor does it require that she earn continuing education points or otherwise meet a specified continuing education requirement. In fact, it is possible that Rose's professional specialty is one in which her skills are best developed through experience. The fact that she keeps her job implies that her level of competence satisfies her employer's requirements and presumably does not violate Rule R4.1. In short, failure to engage in classes, seminars, and workshops does not by itself violate a Rule of professional conduct.

What should Rose do? If the chapter president's report is accurate, Rose should at least consider an attitude adjustment. It is not enough just to pass the

CPCU exams. Professionals should aspire to continuously improving their professional knowledge, skills, and competence. But doing so does not necessarily involve participation in formal classes, seminars, or workshops.

Guideline G2.4 – CPD Program

Beyond the minimum continuing education requirements referred to in Rule R2.1, all CPCUs are urged to engage in such additional pursuits as will meet the aspirational goal, under Canon 2, of *improving* their professional knowledge, skills, and competence.

For example, the Board of Ethical Inquiry suggests that every CPCU should qualify for recognition under the Continuing Professional Development (CPD) program which is jointly sponsored by the American Institute and the CPCU Society.

The CPD program recognizes those who have met specific criteria. The requirements of the CPD program, which are revised from time to time, are automatically distributed to CPCUs who are members of the CPCU Society and are available to others on request. Points are assigned to various activities. Current criteria include:

- Passing an exam or course in a nationally known insurance or business-related program.
- Passing a college or university course in insurance, risk management, or a business-related subject.
- Teaching a course in insurance, risk management, or a business-related subject.
- Authoring or co-authoring an article accepted for publication in the *CPCU Journal* or similar business publication, a CPCU Society section newsletter, or a textbook.
- Conducting a research project.
- Serving as an officer, director, committee chair, or committee member of a national insurance organization or local CPCU chapter.
- Serving as a class coordinator for a CPCU chapter or other course-sponsoring organization.
- Serving on a state insurance advisory committee.
- Grading IIA or CPCU exams.
- Serving on exam development committees for IIA, CPCU, state licensing, or other examination programs.
- Attending the CPCU Annual Meeting and Seminars or the annual meetings of other national insurance organizations.

- Attending educational meetings, seminars, videoconferences, or workshops sponsored by the CPCU Society or others.
- Attending meetings of CPCU chapters or other insurance organizations that include a speaker or an educational program.
- Meeting state continuing education requirements for licensing.
- Being an expert witness.
- Serving as a personal sponsor for CPCU and IIA students.

The CPD program is a voluntary recognition program. It enables CPCUs who record their participation to receive recognition for their activities.

American Institute Position on Continuous Learning for CPCUs

In 1997 the Board of Trustees of the American Institute adopted the following reaffirmation of its earlier position.

1. We reaffirm that the Code of Professional Ethics of the American Institute requires all CPCUs to continue their professional development, as expressed in the Statement on Continuous Learning (below).
2. Because CPCUs are a diverse group with diverse learning needs, we reject the idea of a policing program to determine whether CPCUs have met a defined, measurable minimum standard.
3. We continue to support the Continuing Professional Development (CPD) program, jointly administered by the American Institute and the CPCU Society.
4. We intend to expand Institute services to help CPCUs maintain and enhance their knowledge in a rapidly changing, increasingly complex world.

Statement on Continuous Learning

Continuous learning has always been mandatory for CPCUs subject to the *Code*. *Rule R2.1* under <u>Canon 2</u> of the CPCU *Code of Professional Ethics* requires CPCUs to "<u>keep informed on those technical matters that are essential to the maintenance of the CPCU's professional competence in insurance, risk management, or related fields.</u>" As pointed out in *Guideline G2.1,* "each and every CPCU has an *ethical* obligation to engage actively and continuously in appropriate educational activities."

Although the CPCU Society and the American Institute for CPCU jointly administer a voluntary Continuing Professional Development program, the American Institute has never imposed a mandatory reporting system for determining whether all CPCUs have complied with Rule R2.1. In fact, Guideline G2.2 states that "it is left to the judgment of each CPCU to decide, in light of his or her occupational position, the content and form of continuing education that will satisfy the ethical obligation under *Rule R2.1.*" However, *Guideline G2.3* allows the Board of Ethical Inquiry, while conducting investigations of other alleged violations of the *Code*, to "require the accused to furnish evidence of compliance with *Rule R2.1.*"

Virtually any mandatory system that the American Institute could implement for determining whether CPCUs have complied with *Rule R2.1* would entail the use of an artificial minimum standard. Such a system, by emphasizing an artificial minimum, would serve to undermine the responsibility of each CPCU to identify and pursue "appropriate educational activities."

The following questions and answers address some questions relating to the Institute's position on continuous learning.

Q. Does this mean that continuing education for CPCUs is mandatory or that it is voluntary—or that there is no continuing education requirement at all?

A. Continuous learning that enables CPCUs to fulfill their occupational responsibilities is an ethical requirement, but there is no mandatory system for documenting that all CPCUs have complied with an arbitrary standard.

Q. You say continuous learning is an ethical requirement under the Code of Ethics. The standard (it's up to the individual CPCU) is very subjective. Does that mean this "mandate" is actually unenforceable, and therefore nonexistent?

A. We do the Code a disservice when we overemphasize the enforcement aspects. The primary purpose of the Code of Professional Ethics is to establish high aspirational goals rather than enforcing a minimum standard. However, enforcement may be involved when a CPCU violates a Rule and therefore falls far short of the aspirational goals established in the Canons.

The entire Code of Ethics is enforceable, and CPCUs who fail to comply with any of the Rules can be sanctioned. It is unlikely that a CPCU would be charged with a failure to "maintain and improve knowledge, skills, competence" unless the CPCU's lack of current knowledge has also been reflected through some other violation of the Code.

Q. People *continuously learn* through activities that are not formally counted as *continuing education* because they do not include passing an exam or sitting in a classroom. Are you suggesting that on-the-job experience is enough for most CPCUs? And if you are, doesn't that soften the traditional view that CPCUs should pursue formal courses of study on a continuing basis?

A. Many CPCUs can best maintain professional competence in their occupational responsibilities through seminars, courses, and other formal "education" activities. Others work in a pioneering area for which no book or course has yet been written; their daily work is truly a learning experience. Moreover, professionals use a myriad of informal learning experiences to keep current. The intent is not to soften the importance of formal education, but to acknowledge all types of relevant learning, whether or not they involve time in a classroom. (And sitting in a classroom is not always a learning experience.)

Some jobs provide limited exposure to new ideas. A CPCU who has little opportunity to learn on the job and who makes no effort to learn outside the work environment does not reflect favorably on his or her profession or on the CPCU designation. The Institute would not *initiate* action against a CPCU in such circumstances but would respond to any charges that might be brought under the Code in an appropriate case.

Q. Do CPCUs have a lower standard than insurance agents and brokers who are bound by mandatory continuing education requirements?

A. The Institute provides a credential, not a license. The requirements to earn the CPCU designation are much more stringent than the requirements for obtaining an insurance license. While many insurance licenses require a specified minimum number of continuing education credits, CPCUs have an ethical commitment not only to continuous learning, but also to other provisions of the Code of Professional Ethics of the American Institute.

Q. How does the continuous learning obligation in the Code affect retirees or others who are not currently working in insurance?

A. All CPCUs are obligated to maintain the skills necessary to perform competently in their occupational position. A CPCU who is not active in the insurance/risk management work force would not be required to forfeit the CPCU designation. But on the other hand, he or she would have little reason to use the designation as a credential. When the designation is used, any CPCU should pay heed to Rule R8.2, which requires a CPCU to avoid overstating his or her current level of expertise.

A retired CPCU who, for example, acts as an expert witness in insurance cases, operates as an insurance/risk management consultant, or teaches insurance classes, would be expected to remain informed and competent on those matters with which he or she is involved. A non-retired CPCU who drops out of the work force—for example, because of illness or disability, or to raise a family, or one who shifts to a non-insurance-related career—would not have an ethical obligation to maintain current insurance skills so long as he or she is not active in the insurance business. However, any CPCU returning to the insurance/risk management work force after a long absence would have an ethical obligation to avoid situations that require a more current knowledge than he or she possesses, as well as an obligation to become informed in order to meet current responsibilities.

Q. What about those who became CPCUs before the Code was implemented and who have not voluntarily agreed to be bound by it?

A. Professional standards are not limited to those who have agreed to be bound by the Code. Even before the Code, CPCUs raised their right hands, recited the CPCU Charge (CPCU Professional Commitment), and agreed, among other things, to live by the highest standards of professional conduct. However, it is true that those who are not bound by the Code are not subject to sanctions under the Code.

Q. What is the relationship between the Code of Professional Ethics of the American Institute and the Continuing Professional Development Program?

A. Although both deal with the professional development of CPCUs, there is no direct relationship.

- The Code states the ethical responsibilities of all CPCUs. It also describes a system for censuring those who do not live up to their responsibilities.

- The CPD program is a reward program that provides recognition to CPCUs who have met certain criteria established by the program. The criteria of the CPD program are based in part on the suggestions in Guideline G2.4 of the Code.

Q. What should I tell my clients when they ask what CPCU stands for and whether my CPCU designation means I am *currently* qualified to handle their account because it certifies that I have been keeping up to date?

A. The fact that your ethical commitment to continuous professional development is not monitored does not undermine its value. You may, if you wish, monitor your own educational and developmental activities and maintain records that can be shown to your clients.

Other Related Code Provisions

Canon 2, along with its associated Rules and Guidelines, is closely related to other Code provisions that will be discussed later in greater detail.

- According to Canon 2, CPCUs should "seek continually to maintain and improve their competence." Competence comes up again in Rule R4.1, "A CPCU shall *competently* . . . discharge his or her occupational duties." G4.1 points out that CPCUs maintain their professional competence by keeping informed. Keeping informed results in the competence that is necessary to "consistently discharge . . . occupational duties."

- According to Canon 2, CPCUs should seek continually to maintain and improve their professional knowledge and skills. G6.4 points out that knowledge and skills are necessary for CPCUs to exercise independent judgment *and* to recognize their limitations.

- A professional's current knowledge involves more than the skills required for job performance. G7.2 points out that a CPCU should keep abreast of legislation, changing conditions, and/or other developments that affect the insuring public and should assist in keeping the public informed of them, but CPCUs should also be willing to admit they do not have all the answers.

- G7.3 notes that CPCUs can contribute to a better public understanding of insurance and risk management only if they maintain and improve their own knowledge and communications skills.

- After completing the courses necessary to earn the CPCU designation, CPCUs are ethically obligated to continuous learning. However, R8.2 and G8.2 point out that a CPCU should not give the impression that holding the CPCU designation, by itself, implies a level of knowledge, skills, or capabilities beyond those required to complete the CPCU program.

In short, professional knowledge, skills, and competence do not stand alone, but they provide tools without which a professional cannot fulfill other responsibilities.

Relevant Hypothetical Case Studies

Hypothetical Case Studies appear elsewhere in this publication. The following Hypothetical Case Studies deal in some manner with Canon 2 and related provisions:

- HCS 102
- HCS 104

- HCS 108
- HCS 110
- HCS 112
- HCS 113
- HCS 117

Review Questions

Suggested answers appear elsewhere in this publication.

1. Why is it unethical for a person who does not maintain high levels of professional competence to claim to be a professional?

2. Why is it especially important that you maintain the competence you will develop through your CPCU studies and other professional studies?

3. What is the minimum standard a CPCU should meet in maintaining professional competence?

4. What types of activities will help CPCUs meet the aspirational goal of improving professional knowledge, skills, and competence?

Canon 3 – Legal Conduct

CPCUs should obey all laws and regulations, and should avoid any conduct or activity which would cause unjust harm to others.

The first part of Canon 3 is not an especially lofty goal. Everybody is expected to obey laws and regulations, and failure to do so can lead to legal and administrative sanctions. The second part involves a somewhat loftier objective, stating that CPCUs should avoid any conduct or activity that would cause unjust harm to others. "Unjust harm," is not an accidental redundancy. There is a distinction between harm and unjust harm. Some legal, ethical, and just conduct results in harm to others. For example, if a claim clearly is not covered by its insurance, a claim representative ought to deny payment to a family even if the family is impoverished by the loss for which it cannot recover. To do otherwise would be unjust (see Guideline G1.4).

It is often difficult to recognize—particularly in advance—the ways in which some activity might affect others. Because their studies have exposed them to many facets of insurance and its environment, CPCUs are better equipped than many other practitioners to identify and evaluate the effects of their actions.

To date, every case in which a CPCU's designation has been suspended or revoked has involved a violation of one or more Rules under Canon 3, often in combination with other Rules violations.

Rule R3.1 – Dishonesty, Deceit, Fraud

In the conduct of business or professional activities, a CPCU shall not engage in any act or omission of a dishonest, deceitful, or fraudulent nature.

Dishonesty, deceit, or fraud violate this rule, whether or not they involve the violation of a law or regulation. Each of the following cases in which the Board of Ethical Inquiry (BEI) revoked an individual's CPCU designation involved an alleged violation of Rule 3.1. In most cases other rules were also involved.

- A producer allegedly obtained money under false pretenses by telling an insurance purchaser that the purchaser would be covered by an insurance policy issued by a certain insurance company. The producer admitted in court that he was not an agent for the company, which did not even exist.

- A producer misappropriated premium monies from a consumer. As a result of these charges, his licenses were revoked and he was sentenced to prison. Later, although his CPCU designation had been revoked, upon his release from prison he circulated a resume indicating that he held the CPCU designation. He was then threatened with legal action if he did not cease and desist.

- A producer collected a substantial premium payment from the insured but failed to remit it to the insurer. As a consequence, his license was revoked by the state insurance commissioner.

- A producer misappropriated premium refunds due to policyholders. He consented to revocation of his license and a fine.

- A claim manager awarded repair work in connection with a large number of claims to various building contractors in exchange for a 15 percent kickback. He was convicted on thirteen counts of mail fraud, conspiracy, extortion, and income tax evasion; sentenced to a prison term; and fined.

- A claim adjuster admitted that he had violated the Code by misappropriating funds belonging to his employer through a variety of ruses, including making false claims payments and pocketing the proceeds of salvaged property that was sold.

- A CPCU who served as president of a savings and loan association pled guilty in court to embezzling well over a million dollars from the association.

Because Guideline G3.1 illustrates the types of acts or omissions that might violate both this Rule and the spirit of Canon 3, it is examined next, before we proceed to the next Rule.

Guideline G3.1 – Misrepresentation or Concealment

A CPCU should neither misrepresent nor conceal a fact or information which is material to determining the suitability, efficacy, scope, or limitations of an insurance contract or surety bond. Nor should a CPCU materially misrepresent or conceal the financial condition, or the quality of services, of any insurer or reinsurer. The extent to which a CPCU should volunteer information and facts must necessarily be left to sound professional judgment of what is required under the circumstances. This *Guideline* is intended to illustrate the kinds of acts and omissions which can be "dishonest, deceitful, or fraudulent," in violation of *Rule R3.1,* and which normally "would cause unjust harm to others," thus violating the spirit of *Canon 3.*

Although G3.1 relates most clearly to dishonesty, deceit, or fraud, it may also apply in situations like the following example where the pursuit of financial gain or other personal benefit might get in the way of sound professional judgment—in violation of Rule R3.2, discussed shortly.

Example

In applying for workers compensation insurance, Terri Waite, CPCU, does not mention the fact that one of the raw materials used in her company's manufacturing process releases toxic fumes when exposed to water. In fact, she considers this to be the company's most significant workers compensation exposure.

Has a Rule been violated? The company's most significant workers compensation exposure is certainly material to the insurance contract. Terri's concealment of this information might well constitute dishonesty or deceit, in violation of Rule R3.1. More information would be necessary to judge whether the circumstances made it important for Terri to volunteer information relevant to the hazard. Perhaps the hazard should have been obvious to any involved party, or perhaps the person gathering the information asked no questions at all regarding the extent of the risk.

What should Terri have done? Canon 3 indicates that Terri should avoid any conduct or activity that would cause unjust harm to others. It is likely that the withheld information would have caused harm to the insurance company and, possibly, to employees who might be injured if appropriate loss control measures were not in place. Based on the limited information here, it seems likely that Terri must volunteer the information, both to avoid unjust harm and to avoid any appearance of deceit. Situations like this are invariably much more complex than our brief description here, and simple answers are not necessarily appropriate.

Rule R3.2 – Financial Gain, Personal Benefit

A CPCU shall not allow the pursuit of financial gain or other personal benefit to interfere with the exercise of sound professional judgment and skills.

Many of the most serious charges against CPCUs, including those cited under Rule R3.1, include an alleged violation of Rule R3.2, typically accompanied by other alleged Rule violations. Such charges typically involve the use of money to which the CPCU is not entitled. For example, one CPCU, whose designation has since been revoked, did not return premium refunds to policyholders but retained them for his own benefit. However, R3.2 encompasses not only monetary gain but other personal benefit. Like all Rules, it applies not only to CPCUs but also to CPCU candidates, as illustrated in the next example.

Example

Doug Dooley, a matriculated CPCU candidate, was caught cheating on a CPCU national exam.

Has a Rule been violated? Cheating on an exam, in pursuit of a passing grade, clearly involves dishonesty and deceit, a direct violation of Rule R3.1. The pursuit of personal benefit, in the form of a passing grade on his record, violates R3.2, whether or not Doug would receive a financial reimbursement or reward. As a CPCU candidate, Doug is subject to the Code of Professional Ethics. The Board of Ethical Inquiry would probably suspend Doug's rights to take future CPCU exams.

What should Doug have done? Obviously, Doug should not have cheated on the exam. Instead, he should have done his best to master the material so he could pass it honestly. Cheating is the type of conduct or activity that causes unjust harm to others. It also raises questions regarding Doug's overall moral character and commitment to the principles on which the Code of Professional Ethics is based. If Doug's rights to take future CPCU exams are suspended as a result of this incident, he could, when appropriate, attempt to convince the BEI that he has been rehabilitated and apply for readmission to the CPCU program.

Rule R3.3 – Violation of Law or Regulation; Conviction of a Felony

A CPCU shall not violate any law or regulation relating to professional activities or commit any felony.

R3.3 is the only Rule whose violation may lead to an immediate suspension of the CPCU designation. This information is not included in the body of the Code but in the *Disciplinary Rules, Procedures, and Penalties,* quoted below:

> **A CPCU convicted by verdict, guilty plea, or plea of nolo contendere, of any crime that violates the Rules of Professional Conduct immediately loses the right to use the CPCU designation. Such suspension of the right to use the CPCU designation shall last indefinitely, or until the convicted party petitions the Board of Ethical Inquiry and convinces the Board of that party's fitness again to use the designation.**

Several points are important here. First, automatic suspension applies to conviction of any crime that *violates the Rules of Professional Conduct.* Two crimes fall into this category:

1. Violation of a law relating to *professional* activities
2. Commission of a felony

Notice the position of the phrase "relating to professional activities." CPCUs violate the Code if they commit *any* felony, whether or not it relates to their professional activities. A CPCU who otherwise violates a law or regulation not relating to professional activities is not necessarily in violation of the Code. Unless other Rules are involved, a speeding ticket or a charge of public drunkenness does not provide grounds for action under the Code.

Many CPCUs are subject to regulations promulgated by state insurance departments and other regulatory bodies. Automatic suspension applies to conviction of a crime, not violation of a regulation. A CPCU who violates a regulation relating to professional activities is in violation of Rule R3.3, but that CPCU's designation will not automatically be suspended without further investigation. Guideline G3.3 notes that ignorance is not a defense. CPCUs should be aware of all regulations to which they are subject, and they are obligated to adhere to them. However, the BEI will not sanction a CPCU for violation of a regulation without further investigation and evaluation of the circumstances.

The distinctions among laws, regulations, crimes of different degrees, and professional versus nonprofessional activities can be summarized as follows:

* Violation of an insurance law or regulation relates to professional activities but is not a crime. A candidate or CPCU who violates such laws or regulations may be disciplined, but he or she is not subject to *automatic* suspension.
* Conviction of *any* crime relating to professional activities, including misdemeanors, automatically subjects a candidate or CPCU to immediate suspension.
* Conviction of a felony, whether or not related to professional activities, automatically subjects a candidate to immediate suspension.

Guideline G3.2 – Unfair Competition

A CPCU should not, to the detriment of the insuring public, engage in any business practice or activity designed to restrict fair competition. However, this *Guideline* does not prohibit a CPCU's participation in a legally enforceable covenant not to compete, in a rating bureau, or in a similar activity specifically sanctioned or required by law.

While unfair competition may be illegal, unethical, or both, fair competition is the basis of the free enterprise system. People often disagree as to what competition is fair. Many complex issues and business practices best described in other CPCU courses are part of the insurance business. Insurance is a competitive business, and activities that restrict competition can cause unjust harm to the public. At the same time, some collaborative activities are necessary, legally sanctioned, or required, and they are therefore appropriate. Two examples are given in the Guidelines.

A *covenant not to compete* is a contractual agreement under which one party agrees not to compete with another party. For example, the party selling an insurance agency to a buyer might agree not to engage in insurance sales in the same geographic area as the agency for a stated period of time. Similar contractual agreements are common among independent agents. A new insurance producer, for example, might be required to sign a covenant agreeing not to sell insurance to the same clients, for another agency, within fifty miles for a two-year period after terminating her relationship with her current employer. Although such a covenant restricts a party's rights, it is part of the consideration involved in the contract. A covenant not to compete is generally legal and enforceable, and entering into such a covenant—or enforcing one—does not constitute a violation of the Code. Breach of contract, in violation of a covenant not to compete, might under some circumstances involve violation of one or more Rules of the Code. More often than not, disputes over these covenants—or other civil disputes—involve significant questions of fact and are best resolved by pursuing other remedies. It is not the role of the Code to resolve civil disputes. This point is emphasized in G4.1, discussed later.

Insurance rating bureaus, often called insurance service organizations, maintain a centralized pool of loss data that is used by many insurers in setting their rates. Insurance service organizations also develop standard policy contract forms. All insurance companies using these services might offer a similar product and similar pricing. Some argue that this type of collaboration inhibits fair competition; others believe competition would be limited if insurers did not have the pool of data or standard policy forms on which sound pricing decisions can be based. In any case, rating bureaus are sanctioned or required by law, and mere participation in a rating bureau is not a violation of the Code.

Guideline G3.3 – Inappropriate Compensation

In the performance of the CPCU's own occupational function, a CPCU should not deliberately achieve or seek to achieve, at the expense of the uninformed, financial gains for the CPCU, or the CPCU's employer, which are unconscionable relative to the customary gains for the quantity and quality of services actually rendered.

Generally, no CPCU should seek or accept compensation which is neither for nor commensurate with professional services actually rendered or to be rendered. Nor should any CPCU seek or accept compensation under any other terms, conditions, or circumstances which would violate any *Canon, Guideline,* or *Rule* in this *Code.* However, nothing in this *Guideline* is intended to prohibit the seeking or acceptance of gifts from family or personal friends, income from investments, or income from any other activity which would neither (a) prevent or inherently impair the free and complete exercise of the CPCU's sound professional judgment and skills nor (b) otherwise violate this *Code.*

A CPCU should not perform professional services under terms, conditions, or circumstances which would prevent or inherently impair the free and complete exercise of the CPCU's sound professional judgment and skills. This guideline does not prohibit a CPCU from being compensated under the terms of a legally acceptable commission arrangement since such an arrangement, in itself, does not prevent or inherently impair the CPCU's sound professional judgment and skills. But it does serve to remind a CPCU so compensated of his or her ethical obligation to avoid any recommendation to a consumer of the CPCU's services that would increase the CPCU's compensation, unless such recommendation clearly meets the consumer's legitimate needs and best interests. The guideline also serves to remind every CPCU, regardless of his or her basis of compensation, of the ethical obligation to render fully such services as are contemplated and rightfully owed under the terms of the applicable compensation arrangement.

CPCUs should not overcharge for their services. People might have vastly different opinions as to what a person's services are worth, but the Guideline makes it clear that "unconscionable" charges, well outside the customary charges for similar services, are inappropriate—especially if they seek to take advantage of an uninformed consumer.

It is inappropriate to solicit or accept bribes in exchange for a favor, whether that favor involves paying a claim, accepting an application, or performing other services. However, it is obviously appropriate to accept birthday presents and other gifts from family members and friends, and it is even appropriate to expect them. G3.3 emphasizes the fact that inappropriate compensation or gifts should not in any way affect a CPCU's judgment or skills. In fact, a CPCU should not perform professional services under circumstances where his or her professional judgment is constrained.

G3.3 also makes it clear that while commission income (reimbursement as a percentage of sales) is appropriate, CPCUs ought to avoid recommendations that would increase the CPCU's income unless the recommendation also clearly serves the customer's best interests.

Guideline G3.4 – Awareness of Applicable Laws and Regulations

While the Institute's standards of ethical conduct are by no means limited to the duties and obligations imposed upon CPCUs by the laws and regulations which govern the conduct of all insurance practitioners, obedience to and respect for law and regulatory authority should be viewed as an absolute minimum standard of professional conduct below which no CPCU should fall. The potential consequences of violating this admonition extend beyond those which may fall upon the violator, since one CPCU may indeed bring discredit upon the CPCU designation, and thus all who hold it, by violating laws or regulations which govern the conduct of a CPCU's business activities.

A CPCU is obligated to keep fully informed of each and every law and regulation governing or otherwise pertaining to his business activities. In so doing, a CPCU should not hesitate to seek interpretive assistance from the appropriate regulatory officials and/or retain the services of competent legal counsel. When in doubt as to the legality of a particular kind of business conduct or activity, the CPCU should refrain from such conduct or activity.

A CPCU may not plead lack of knowledge as a defense for improper conduct under *Rule R3.3* unless the CPCU can demonstrate that he or she had made a reasonable effort in good faith to obtain such knowledge, and it was not available.

Legal requirements provide a minimum standard, and violation of R3.3 may lead to automatic suspension as discussed earlier. As G3.4 suggests, a CPCU who violates laws or regulations is an embarrassment to all CPCUs. It is not uncommon, when a CPCU is charged with or convicted of some violation, for an officer of the local CPCU chapter to promptly contact the Ethics Counsel and initiate a complaint so the offender can be disciplined, if such an action is applicable, and removed from the rolls of the CPCU chapter as quickly as possible, before causing further embarrassment.

Other Related Code Provisions

Canon 3, along with its associated Rules and Guidelines, is closely related to other Code provisions, including several that will be discussed later in greater detail.

- Obedience to laws and regulations, and avoiding unjust activity, clearly relates to the precepts of Canon 1, placing the public interest above one's own.
- R1.2 makes it clear that any CPCU who does not personally violate R3.1, R3.2, or R3.3 but condones others' violations is in violation of the Code.

- To avoid breaking a law or violating a regulation, CPCUs must keep informed, as indicated in Canon 2 and R2.1.

- Avoiding any conduct or activity which would cause unjust harm to others can best be done by a person who has the knowledge, skills, and competence necessary to recognize the implications of his or her actions. This requires "keeping informed" through "continuous learning," in keeping with Canon 2 and R2.1.

Relevant Hypothetical Case Studies

Hypothetical Case Studies appear elsewhere in this publication. The following Hypothetical Case Studies deal in some manner with Canon 3 and related provisions:

- HCS 101
- HCS 102
- HCS 103
- HCS 104
- HCS 105
- HCS 106
- HCS 107
- HCS 109
- HCS 110
- HCS 111
- HCS 113
- HCS 114
- HCS 115
- HCS 116
- HCS 117
- HCS 118
- HCS 119
- HCS 122

Review Questions

Suggested answers appear elsewhere in this publication.

1. Naturally, CPCUs are expected not to engage in illegal activities, but legality is generally considered a minimum standard of behavior. How do the aspirational goals of Canon 3 go beyond encouraging legal behavior?

2. Are CPCUs subject to discipline for illegal conduct outside the scope of their business conduct? Explain.

3. Under what circumstances is a CPCU to be held responsible for violating a law or regulation he or she did not know about?

Canon 4 – Diligent Performance

CPCUs should be diligent in the performance of their occupational duties and should continually strive to improve the functioning of the insurance mechanism.

There are two parts to this Canon. The first reflects behavior *on the job,* and the second involves a CPCU's effect on the risk management and insurance *environment.* These two parts are reflected in the two Rules that fall under Canon 4. R4.1 addresses occupational duties, while R4.2 deals with improving the insurance mechanism.

Are these two parts related? Sometimes. The work of some CPCUs has a direct effect on the insurance environment. Examples include those involved in product development, research, or regulation. The day-to-day activities of other CPCUs have little direct effect on the insurance mechanism as a whole, but they should still be performed with diligence.

CPCU candidates who are near the beginning of their careers might think it unlikely that they could have any personal impact on "improving the insurance mechanism." But as their careers progress, many current candidates will reach highly influential positions in insurance, risk management, or related fields—positions that can literally change the insurance world, or at least influence change.

Perhaps it goes without saying that CPCUs, like other people, should perform their jobs with diligence and should strive to make the world a better place. Unfortunately, competing interests, selfishness, and other factors sometimes get in the way. These are addressed in the Rules.

Rule R4.1 – Performing Occupational Duties

A CPCU shall competently and consistently discharge his or her occupational duties.

Guideline G4.1 will be discussed next because it is directly linked to this Rule. Some of the guidance in G4.1 is also relevant to other areas of the Code.

Guideline G4.1 – Employment, Contractual, and Civil Disputes Involving Diligent Performance

From one who purports to be a true professional, the public has a right to expect both competence, in the sense of abilities, and diligent performance, in the sense of consistently applying those abilities in the service of others.

Thus, to complement *Rule R2.1,* which obligates a CPCU to maintain professional competence by keeping informed, the Institute also promulgated *Rule R4.1,* which stipulates that "a CPCU shall competently and consistently *discharge* his or her occupational duties."

Although the Board of Ethical Inquiry earnestly believes that diligent performance should be an ethical obligation of all professionals, including CPCUs, the Board will not intervene or arbitrate between the parties in an employment or contractual relationship or civil dispute. Nor does the Board feel that the Institute's disciplinary procedures should become a substitute for legal and other remedies available to such parties. In the event of an alleged violation of *Rule R4.1,* therefore, the Board will hear the case only after all other remedies have been exhausted, and it generally will take disciplinary action only under circumstances where (1) a proven violation has caused unjust harm to another person, and the violation brings substantial discredit upon the CPCU designation; or (2) it would otherwise be in the *public* interest to take disciplinary action under the ethics code.

Relationship Between Continuous Learning and Competent Performance

Notice the direct relationship between Rule R2.1 and Rule R4.1. A professional cannot competently discharge his or her duties without also keeping informed of all factors that affect those duties. In discussing Rule R2.1, we noted that a CPCU probably would not be sanctioned under the Code merely for failure to keep up to date. But failure to keep current is inevitably reflected in job performance, and when that happens a CPCU might violate both R4.1 and R2.1. Keeping current is one important way to prevent violating R4.1.

Employment Relationships, Contractual Relationships, Civil Disputes

The authors of the Code recognized that the disciplinary actions for violating the ethical obligation of diligent performance had to be qualified in carefully drafted Guidelines, so that the Institute would not become an intervenor or arbitrator in contractual or civil disputes with employers, principals, or clients.[4] G4.1 makes it clear that *the Code of Ethics is not a remedy for employer-employee disputes, nor is it a remedy for other disputes that can better be settled through legal procedures and other remedies.* The BEI will not become involved in such disputes until other remedies have been exhausted.

Diligent performance of occupational duties is desirable, of course, but determining what constitutes "diligent performance" can be highly subjective,

---

4. Ronald C. Horn, *On Professions, Professionals, and Professional Ethics* (Malvern, PA: American Institute for Property and Liability Underwriters, 1st ed., 1978), p. 98.

especially when promotions, performance evaluations, salary adjustments, and other elements of the work environment are involved. Interpersonal disputes, whether or not they involve employment, contracts, or civil law, often generate heated emotions. A person who feels wronged wants to lash out against the alleged wrongdoer in every way possible. It is not unusual for this lashing-out to take the form of an ethics complaint.

A disciplinary action does not fix problems like these. Other remedies are better suited and more effective in resolving problems in these categories. If a contract has been breached, the more effective remedy is to seek to enforce the contract, not to seek a reprimand or other action from the Board of Ethical Inquiry.

Example

Paul Jones signed a covenant not to compete when he accepted his job as an insurance producer for the ABC insurance agency. After working for ABC for five years, learning the ropes, earning his CPCU designation, and gaining a number of accounts for ABC, Paul gets a better offer and goes to work for DEF Insurance Agency. Many of Paul's clients transfer their business to DEF. Henry Crow, CPCU, one of ABC's principals, complains to the Board of Ethical Inquiry that Paul has violated his covenant not to compete and stands in violation of R4.1.

As is typical, there are two sides to the story. ABC contends that Paul breached the contractual agreement in his covenant not to compete. Paul contends that strict enforcement of the covenant would constitute an unfair restraint of trade and that while he did not solicit the business, "his clients" made the choice to continue doing business with Paul, even if doing so involved a different agency.

Has a Rule been violated? As indicated in connection with G3.3, entering into or enforcing a covenant not to compete does not violate the Rules under Canon 3. The BEI would not hear this case until other remedies had been resolved. Even then, the BEI generally would not take action unless unjust harm has been caused to another person, the CPCU designation has been discredited, or disciplinary action would be in the public interest. Under such circumstances, perhaps another Rule has also been violated.

Likewise, the BEI would not get involved in any countercharges from Paul suggesting that Henry Crow had violated R4.1 by engaging in unfair competition.

Henry Crow has not violated a Rule by filing an ethics complaint without first seeking a remedy under contract law.

Although it appears no Rule has been violated by either party, another factor should, perhaps, be considered. In this case, as with many employment-related disputes, the professional relationship between Henry and Paul might have deteriorated to one that is less than "dignified and honorable," which at least violates the spirit of Canon 6 (discussed later).

What should they do? Paul and Henry should attempt to resolve their dispute between themselves. If that is not possible, it might become necessary to involve the legal system, filing a lawsuit as a last resort. The outcome will depend on the facts of the case and any legal principles that are applied. Once their dispute is resolved, Paul and Henry will probably go about their business as friendly—or not-so-friendly—competitors. Disputes of this type are common and usually result from other factors, not a choice to act in a way that is contrary to the public interest. In rare cases, the proceedings might identify a serious ethical breach that would be considered by the BEI, but only after other remedies have been pursued to a reasonable conclusion.

One might argue that the example above did not directly involve "occupational duties." Because it is presented in connection with Canon 4, G4.1 applies most specifically to the performance of occupational duties. However, the principle discussed in G4.1 applies to other types of activities as well. *The enforcement provisions of the Code of Ethics are not an appropriate substitute for legal remedies or other remedies that are available in many cases.*

Rule R4.2 – Improving the Insurance Mechanism

A CPCU shall support efforts to effect such improvements in claims settlement, contract design, investment, marketing, pricing, reinsurance, safety engineering, underwriting, and other insurance operations as will both inure to the benefit of the public and improve the overall efficiency with which the insurance mechanism functions.

How are CPCUs expected to support efforts to improve the insurance mechanism? Examples are given in the Guidelines that focus on policy language, financial integrity, availability, efficiency, humanitarianism, and support for research. These are only examples. CPCUs' efforts to improve risk management and insurance certainly are not limited to these areas.

Improving the Insurance Mechanism; G4.2 and Related Guidelines

Guideline G4.2 appears below. Because Guidelines G4.3 through G4.8 clarify the principles in G4.2, they are also discussed under this heading.

In addition to competently and consistently discharging his or her own occupational duties, a CPCU is obligated by *Rule R4.2* "to support efforts to effect such improvements (in insurer functions and operations) as will both inure to the benefit of the public and improve the overall efficiency with which the insurance mechanism functions." Note that the obligation is to support the kinds of improvements which will *both* improve the efficiency of the insurance mechanism *and* benefit the public. The drafters of the *Code* worded the rule in this fashion to focus attention on the fact that it is possible to effect improvements in insurer efficiency and profitability at least in the short run, in a manner contrary to the public interest. Granted, it is sometimes very difficult to determine whether a proposed change will both improve overall efficiency and inure to the benefit of the public, but the ethical obligation, consistent with the theme expressed in *Canon 1*, is to support *efforts* to effect such improvements. The kinds of efforts which satisfy both criteria, and which the Board feels a CPCU should support, are illustrated in the *Guidelines* immediately following.

The principles in G4.2 are clarified in Guidelines G4.3 through G4.8. Further discussion follows the wording of G4.8.

Guideline G4.3 – Policy Language
A CPCU should assist in improving the language, suitability, adaptability, and general efficacy of insurance contracts and surety bonds.

Guideline G4.4 – Financial Integrity
A CPCU should assist in ensuring protection and security for the public, and in maintaining and improving the integrity of the insurance institution, by helping to preserve and improve the financial strength of all private insurers.

Guideline G4.5 – Availability
A CPCU should assist in providing an adequate supply of insurance and surety bonds to meet public demands and needs.

Guideline G4.6 – Efficiency
A CPCU should do the utmost to assist in minimizing the cost to the public of insurance and suretyship, without compromising the quality of benefits or services they provide, not only by helping to improve the operational efficiency of insurers and their representatives but also by contributing to the solution of economic, legal, political, and other social problems which demonstrably increase the cost of insurance and suretyship without enhancing their quality or otherwise improving the public well-being. Ex-

amples of such problems include, though are not limited to, inflation, unemployment, crime, inequities and inefficiencies in our legal system, inequities
and inefficiencies in our health care delivery system, riots, floods and other
highly destructive natural catastrophes, and the physical deterioration of
property in the nation's cities. The ready availability of insurance alone will
not solve such problems. And a CPCU should not neglect his or her personal duty, as a good citizen and a professional, to become actively involved
in the search for underlying causes of, and long-run solutions to, such
problems.

Guideline G4.7 – Humanitarianism and Loss Control

Because of a CPCU's professional capabilities and firsthand knowledge of
the tragic magnitude of human and dollar losses suffered annually, a CPCU
should assume an especially active role in private and public loss prevention
and reduction efforts. A CPCU should do the utmost to preserve each and
every human life, maintain and improve the physical and mental health of
all human beings, and prevent the damage, destruction, and abstraction of
property.

Guideline G4.8 – Support for Research

A CPCU should make an effort to participate in and support research
which promises to assist in improving the functioning of the private insurance mechanism and/or in reducing losses of life, health, or property.

As educated insurance professionals, CPCUs are in a position to have a posi-
tive influence on the "insurance mechanism." CPCUs who are in leadership
positions within the insurance industry play major roles in improving the
insurance mechanism. But every CPCU can play at least a small part. CPCUs
often can serve to:

- improve insurance and surety contracts,
- maintain the financial strength and integrity of risk financing systems,
- help ensure the availability of insurance, surety bonds, and alternative
  risk financing systems,
- improve efficiency and otherwise help minimize the cost of insurance
  and other so-called costs of risk,
- play an important role in loss prevention and loss reduction efforts, and
- support research in the areas mentioned above.

Like motherhood and apple pie, the things required by R4.2 are clearly good to
support. In fact, they are so obvious that R4.2 might seem unnecessary. How
then might one violate Rule R4.2? By supporting self-serving changes to the

insurance mechanism that do not inure to the benefit of the public or improvements of the insurance mechanism, or by working to prevent changes that would benefit the public interest.

Wise, well-educated, well-informed people—including CPCUs—are likely to have widely varying opinions regarding the effect of proposed changes. In fact, some CPCUs have given strong public support to issues that others oppose. While not specifically mentioned in the Guidelines that relate to improving the insurance mechanism, it seems unlikely that the BEI would become involved in an ethics action based primarily on a difference in opinion regarding some proposed change, unless it were unequivocally shown that the CPCU's position is based on personal gain at the expense of the public.

Guideline G4.9 – Individual Participation in Political or Governmental Activities

The ethical obligation under this *Code* to strive for improvement in the functioning of the private insurance mechanism does not bar a CPCU from serving in the public sector. Nor does it bar a CPCU, as an *individual* citizen, from supporting a governmental role in providing economic security for the citizenry. But a CPCU should be mindful of the restriction imposed by Rule R8.4, and should avoid even the appearance of speaking on behalf of the Institute, especially on political matters.

Three important, related issues are discussed in G4.9. First, are CPCUs prohibited from serving in the public sector in elected, appointed, volunteer, or advisory positions? Of course not. A number of CPCUs have served as state insurance commissioners or held other political offices. CPCUs have even served as state governors. Most CPCUs understand the insurance mechanism much better than most members of the public. By becoming involved in public-sector activities, CPCUs can play a valuable role in improving the insurance mechanism.

It is no secret that politicians, regulators, lobbyists, and others in the public sector have frequently been the target of "ethics violations" as that term is generally understood, often arising from conflicts of interest. CPCUs engaged in public sector activities should be especially cautious to support activities that would serve to improve the insurance mechanism and best serve the public interest, and to place the public interest above their own. Often, private interests also benefit from activities that benefit the public. For example, private insurance companies and the public both benefited from the "write your own" program under which private insurers could offer flood insurance underwritten by the federal government. However, CPCUs should be cautious that private interests do not outweigh the public interest.

Although CPCUs are required to "support efforts" that improve insurance, these efforts are not always successful. R4.2 requires effort, not success.

Example

Following a court decision favorable to persons injured in auto accidents, auto insurance losses soared in the fictitious state of West Carolina. The West Carolina insurance commissioner, a CPCU, refused to grant rate increases on the basis that this would make insurance unaffordable. Instead, he urged the state legislature to pass a law overriding the court decision. Meanwhile, with his bid for re-election coming up soon, he issued an administrative order prohibiting insurance companies from canceling auto policies currently in force. Susan Smith, CPCU, president of ABC Insurance Company, a regional company doing business primarily in West Carolina, immediately ordered all ABC underwriters to stop accepting new business. Susan also wrote a letter to all CPCU chapter presidents in the state, urging them to support ABC's action and filed a formal complaint with the BEI, alleging that the commissioner had violated Rules R4.1 and R4.2. Meanwhile, agents in West Carolina filed an ethics complaint against Susan Jones, alleging that her actions in closing the market were in violation of R4.1 and R4.2.

Has a Rule been violated? The answer to this question would not be clear without further investigation, and even then it might be strictly a matter of opinion, rather than fact. Let's examine the issues. The discussion here is limited to R4.1 and R4.2, although other Rules might also be considered:

- The commissioner is attempting to keep insurance affordable. This is appropriate under R4.2.

- The commissioner is proposing legislation to keep insurance affordable. This, too, is in keeping with R4.2.

- The commissioner's administrative order keeps insurance available. Availability is in keeping with R4.2, but requiring insurance companies to write business at a loss hardly serves to improve the functioning of the insurance mechanism.

- The upcoming election suggests that the commissioner is placing his own interests (getting reelected) above the public interest. If he gets the vote, the public presumably assumes its interests have been protected.

- Assuming no veiled threats are involved because of her influential position in the insurance market, Susan Smith would not violate R4.2 by writing to CPCU chapter presidents and encouraging them, as individuals, to agree with her position. It would also be appropriate for CPCU chapter presidents to discuss the issues as the topic of a chapter meeting.

However, the CPCU Society as an organization does not take a position on political issues (based on the Society's own rules, not the Code of Professional Ethics of the American Institute).

- In refusing to accept new business, Susan Smith might reduce the availability of insurance in West Carolina (depending on the rest of the market). However, this move also helps preserve ABC's financial integrity. Susan might argue that this is indeed a discharge of her occupational duties.

This example illustrates the difficulty involved in adhering to the Rules under Canon 4, and it also demonstrates the challenges the BEI might face in evaluating complaints. In most cases, the BEI would rely on other mechanisms to resolve complaints such as these–which are heavily based on opinions as to what constitutes an improvement of the insurance mechanism. However, action might be taken under circumstances mentioned in G4.1: "(1) a proven violation has caused unjust harm to another person, and the violation brings substantial discredit upon the CPCU designation; or (2) it would otherwise be in the *public* interest to take disciplinary action under the ethics code."

What should they have done? To live up to the high aspirational goals of Canon 4, all parties should be diligent in the performance of their occupational duties and continually strive to improve the functioning of the insurance mechanism. The circumstances of this case describe some malfunctions of the insurance mechanism. However, they might be outside the control of the CPCUs involved. Indeed, it appears that these CPCUs were striving to effect improvements. Unfortunately, trying does not always equal succeeding.

CPCUs may act as individuals in "supporting a governmental role" in insurance- and risk-related activities. For example, a CPCU is not barred from writing a letter to a state representative or regulator expressing his or her views on pending legislation. However, the CPCU should not imply that he or she is speaking for other CPCUs, or for the American Institute for CPCU, in expressing an opinion.

A related question is whether a CPCU, when acting as an individual, should use his or her designation when writing a letter or article dealing with public-sector activities. If Chris Kraus is writing to encourage her state representative to vote against a bill, should she sign the letter "Chris Kraus, CPCU"? If she is writing a letter to the editor, or an article for publication, should she include her designation? The answer to both questions is yes. Each question illustrates an appropriate use of the designation. However, Chris should not imply that she is expressing the view of other CPCUs or of the American Institute.

Incidentally, Chris might invite other CPCUs to add their signatures to her letter, and that also would be appropriate, so long as no coercion is involved and it is clear that all CPCUs are expressing an individual opinion and not suggesting that they speak for a larger group.

Why the concern? CPCUs are a diverse group with many different perspectives. There are few issues, if any, over which all CPCUs are in agreement, and it would be inappropriate—and unethical—to suggest otherwise.

Other Related Code Provisions

Striving to improve the functioning of the insurance mechanism might involve various activities that seek to influence others, such as writing articles or public speaking, to which the following items relate:

- R2.1 complements R4.1 by emphasizing the fact that keeping informed is an essential element of competence.

- G5.2 emphasizes the point that, when writing or speaking publicly as a CPCU, a CPCU should maintain the dignity and high professional standards appropriate to the designation.

- According to G7.6, CPCUs are not required to support lobbying efforts or proposed legislation, nor are they required to take positions on controversial issues.

- G7.6 and R8.4 also make it clear that CPCUs may engage in lobbying activities, support proposed legislation, or take a position on controversial issues, providing each CPCU does so as an individual and does not appear to speak on behalf of the American Institute.

Relevant Hypothetical Case Studies

Hypothetical Case Studies appear elsewhere in this publication. The Rules under Canon 4 are considered in the following Hypothetical Case Studies:

- HCS 103
- HCS 105
- HCS 107
- HCS 111
- HCS 112
- HCS 113
- HCS 116
- HCS 117
- HCS 118

Review Question

A suggested answer appears elsewhere in this publication.

In what ways should a CPCU use his or her knowledge and skills in improving the insurance mechanism?

Canon 5 – Maintaining and Raising Professional Standards

CPCUs should assist in maintaining and raising professional standards in the insurance business.

The first three Rules under this Canon involve getting competent people into the business and encouraging their growth, as well as fostering competence and ethical conduct. The last rule addresses professional standards in a different way. Basically, CPCUs are required to cooperate with regulatory authorities when an insurance practitioner's conduct comes into question. (The Board of Ethical Inquiry is not a regulatory authority. Rule R9.2, discussed later, discusses CPCUs' participation in ethics investigations by the American Institute.)

Rule R5.1 – Bring Qualified People into the Business

A CPCU shall support personnel policies and practices which will attract qualified individuals to the insurance business, provide them with ample and equal opportunities for advancement, and encourage them to aspire to the highest levels of professional competence and achievement.

Rule R5.2 – Assist Others in Pursuing CPCU and Other Studies

A CPCU shall encourage and assist qualified individuals who wish to pursue CPCU or other studies which will enhance their professional competence.

Rule R5.3 – Support Measures to Foster Competence and Ethical Conduct

A CPCU shall support the development, improvement, and enforcement of such laws, regulations, and codes as will foster competence and ethical conduct on the part of all insurance practitioners and inure to the benefit of the public.

Rule R5.4 – Support Regulatory Investigations

A CPCU shall not withhold information or assistance officially requested by appropriate regulatory authorities who are investigating or prosecuting any alleged violation of the laws or regulations governing the qualifications or conduct of the insurance business.

Guidelines

Two Guidelines discuss the application of Canon 5 and the four related Rules.

Guideline G5.1 – Setting an Example

A CPCU should assist in the raising of professional standards in the insurance business. At a minimum, every CPCU should conduct his or her own business activities in a manner which will, by the CPCU's precept and example, inspire other practitioners to do likewise.

Because the Rules under Canon 5 emphasize "other people," it is easy to overlook the fact that Canon 5 includes maintaining one's own professional standards. G5.1 reminds CPCUs that they ought to set an example through the standards on which their own professional conduct is based.

Guideline G5.2 – Encouraging Others' Professional Development

Both the insuring public and the insurance industry will benefit from continued growth in the number of insurance practitioners who achieve a high level of professional attainment. Thus, Rule R5.2 stipulates that "A CPCU shall encourage and assist qualified individuals who wish to pursue CPCU or other studies which will enhance their professional competence."

CPCUs are ethically obligated to encourage other qualified persons to pursue CPCU and other studies. Another Guideline, related directly to Canon 9, emphasizes the importance of quality. According to G9.1, "it is not an objective of the American Institute to achieve growth in the number of CPCUs at the expense of professional standards, but rather to encourage more, qualified individuals to meet the high standards which have always characterized the CPCU designation requirements." As Dr. Harry J. Loman, the Institute's first dean, put it in 1942: "The [CPCU] program was not designed for every person connected with the insurance business but only for those who could pass [originally] five comprehensive examinations at the senior college level and would agree to conduct their business in accordance with high professional standards."[5] CPCUs should attempt to identify more "qualified individuals with high standards," people who would make good CPCUs, and encourage them to pursue the CPCU designation. It would not be appropriate to blindly encourage every insurance practitioner to become a CPCU.

A CPCU should share with all other insurance practitioners, as well as fellow CPCUs, the benefits of the CPCU's professional attainments. A CPCU's

---

5. Harry J. Loman, "The C.P.C.U. Dream," *CPCU Annals*, December 1970, p. 301.

conduct should be guided by a spirit of altruistic concern for the public interest, and the public interest is best served when all insurance practitioners are well informed.

Moreover, any professional who has acquired a unified body of knowledge is invariably indebted to innumerable predecessors and contemporaries for having made available the benefits of their professional attainments, that is, for having shared freely with others their knowledge, accumulated experiences, skills, and insights into understanding. So also should a CPCU, as a professional who has subscribed to high ethical standards, share freely with contemporaries and, thus, future generations, the benefits of his or her own professional attainments, apart from any hope or expectation of immediate financial gain, because of the CPCU's ethical obligations to repay an indebtedness to forebears, contribute to the efficient advancement of human knowledge, and manifest an altruistic concern for the public interest.

In varying ways, the preceding two paragraphs point out that CPCUs, like other professionals, ought to share their expertise with others rather than keeping it to themselves. CPCUs ought to share their expertise with future generations, just as previous generations have made it possible for them to gain their own expertise. Many CPCUs have become CPCU/IIA course leaders; others lead CPCU Society or other seminars, engage in research projects, write textbooks, grade exams, or serve in various volunteer roles because they feel a duty to "pass it along." Indeed, it is a duty.

A CPCU should support and participate in educational activities which will assist other practitioners in their professional development. Examples of such activities include seminars, lectures, research projects, teaching, preparation of educational materials for training programs, and preparation of professional articles for professional or lay publications. In writing or speaking publicly as a CPCU, however, the CPCU should maintain the dignity and high professional standards appropriate to the designation.

The authors of the Code debated stronger wording that would *obligate* CPCUs to share the benefits of their professional attainments with other insurance practitioners. Opponents felt that such a rule would obligate CPCUs to divulge trade secrets and knowledge that give them a competitive advantage. The compromise wording requires CPCUs *to support efforts* to improve the public understanding of insurance and risk management—and to do so with the dignity associated with the CPCU tradition.[6] Although CPCUs have an ethical obligation to share the benefits of their knowledge, there is a distinc-

---

6. Ronald C. Horn, *On Professions, Professionals, and Professional Ethics* (Malvern, PA: American Institute for Property and Liability Underwriters, 1st ed., 1978), p. 98.

tion between sharing basic knowledge and divulging trade secrets. The final paragraph clarifies any possible misunderstanding on this point.

This *Guideline* does not obligate a CPCU to divulge trade secrets or other information which would put the CPCU at a competitive disadvantage. Instead, it serves as a reminder that just as the truly professional physician demonstrates a commitment to the advancement of medicine by sharing his or her knowledge and experiences with other physicians and aspiring physicians, so also should a CPCU play a role in the development of the field of insurance, in part by sharing knowledge with other practitioners as well as students.

Example

Art Raymond, CPCU, is the Branch Manager in charge of the Lima office of Succotash Insurance Company. His leadership role strongly influences the careers of the 200 people employed in this office. Although Art pays CPCU chapter dues, he never attends chapter meetings, and no employees in his office are pursuing the CPCU designation. A member of the chapter's Candidate Recruitment and Development Committee tells Art that his failure to support CPCU activities is a violation of his ethical responsibilities under Rules R5.1 and R5.2 of the Code of Ethics. Art responds that he has no time for CPCU activities and directs his employees to spend their time on production rather than study.

Has a Rule been broken? First, regarding Art's own level of CPCU activity, although active CPCU members find that chapter activities help them live up to the goals of the Canons, there is no Rule requiring CPCUs to join the CPCU Society or be active in it. G5.1 notes that Art, like all CPCUs, should set a good example, but failure to do so, by itself, does not violate a Rule.

Not only is Art an inactive CPCU. He also deprives others—the employees in his office—from the opportunities to advance by pursuing CPCU or other studies. Unfortunately, Art's statement might reflect a higher-level management decision over which he has no control. Otherwise, Art's strong position on this issue is a direct violation of Rule R5.1.

What should Art do? All CPCUs should assist in maintaining and raising professional standards in the insurance business. Where he has an influence on company policy, Art is ethically obligated to support policies that help employees get ahead. He should also encourage and assist those individuals who are qualified to take CPCU courses, or other courses, that aid in their professional development.

Other Related Code Provisions

Other Code provisions also relate to the matter of maintaining and raising professional standards in the insurance business.

- Supervisors and others whose occupational duties involve others' career development should consider their aspirational duties under Canon 4, as well as their obligations under the related Rules. Sometimes persons in a leadership position cannot diligently perform their occupational duties unless they encourage their employees' professional development.
- G7.6 includes guidelines on lobbying, or other activities, in which a CPCU might engage while meeting his or her R5.3 obligations to support legislation and regulation that foster competence and ethical conduct in insurance.
- While R5.4 requires CPCUs to cooperate with investigations by regulatory authorities, R9.2 requires CPCUs to cooperate with the American Institute in any investigation of an ethics complaint.
- R5.3, R5.4, and R9.2 do not require a CPCU to report illegal or unethical behavior. In fact, R6.2 and G6.6 indicate that CPCUs should use caution and sound judgment when dealing with confidential information.
- G9.1 underscores the importance of professional standards, and of encouraging qualified individuals to meet them, by pointing out that it is not the American Institute's goal to sacrifice standards in order to increase the number of CPCUs.

Relevant Hypothetical Case Studies

Hypothetical Case Studies appear elsewhere in this publication. The Rules under Canon 5 are considered in the following Hypothetical Case Studies:

- HCS 101
- HCS 108
- HCS 111
- HCS 114

Review Question

A suggested answer appears elsewhere in this publication.

Is a CPCU obligated under the Code to answer all questions posed by appropriate regulatory authorities investigating other CPCUs' conduct?

Canon 6 – Professional Relationships

CPCUs should strive to establish and maintain dignified and honorable relationships with those whom they serve, with fellow insurance practitioners, and with members of other professions.

This Canon involves CPCUs' relationships with three groups of people:

- Their customers (those whom they serve)
- Fellow insurance practitioners
- Members of other professions

What types of relationships should CPCUs strive to establish and maintain? The ideal relationship should be both dignified and honorable. The insurance business has long been characterized as a business of utmost good faith. The very nature of most insurance transactions requires that a strong element of trust be part of both the image and the reality of an insurance or risk management professional.

Rule R6.1 – Legal Limitations

A CPCU shall keep informed on the legal limitations imposed upon the scope of his or her professional duties.

What might those legal limitations be? That depends, of course, on both the nature of the CPCU's duties and the laws affecting those duties. For example, claim representatives, as well as others involved in the claim process, should not engage in the unauthorized practice of law. Likewise, they should follow any unfair claims practices acts to which they are subject. Insurance advisors should not give advice that requires a securities license unless they have one. Underwriters, producers, and others are subject to unfair trade practices acts that include such touchy topics as unfair discrimination. Licensed practitioners are subject to the regulatory provisions associated with their license. Whatever their professional duties, CPCUs are expected to know their legal limitations.

Rule R6.2 – Confidential Information

A CPCU shall not disclose to another person any confidential information entrusted to, or obtained by, the CPCU in the course of the CPCU's business or professional activities, unless a disclosure of such information is required by law or is made to a person who necessarily must have the information in order to discharge legitimate occupational or professional duties.

In the normal course of business, people in insurance and risk management have access to a tremendous amount of confidential information—information that is necessary for the business to operate. Insurance files are filled with information on individuals' health, income, and reputation. Insurers accumulate data on businesses that includes profit information, secret ingredients, business plans, products hazards, and other proprietary information and trade secrets. This information is entrusted to insurers because it is necessary to do business and because there is an implicit agreement that the information will be held in confidence.

Confidentiality

"It's always interesting for me to listen to others talk about what they think is not confidential. I'm amazed at information that I receive which has no appearance of being considered confidential yet is extraordinarily revealing. Some facts are inappropriate for discussion because they provide business references of others that may be out of bounds for discussion."

—Insurance company chairman of the board

A 1997 study, conducted by researchers at Oregon State University and funded by the Insurance Institute for Applied Ethics,[7] revealed that little legislation governs the use of personal information gathered by insurance companies. However, it encourages the insurance industry to recognize that:

- The privacy concerns of its customers are legitimate, and appropriate steps should be taken to secure data.
- Careful data handling can be a competitive advantage. (If you do it well, take credit for it.)
- Almost every activity of insurers, agents, and trade organizations can have secondary effects that deal with data and privacy.
- Rules governing the privacy of data will evolve from social values and will eventually produce a body of common law.
- Society harbors an inherent distrust of large organizations, including insurers. That distrust, in turn, implies that regulation of the insurance industry's data practices is a real possibility. One strategy to avoid unacceptable regulations is to work to develop a system that will provide the regulation.

Because Guideline G6.6 relates specifically to this Rule, it is discussed next, before R6.3.

---

7. Daniel J. Brown, Linda Gamill, Norma L. Nielson, Mary Alice Seville, *Ethical Uses of Information in Insurance* (Malvern, PA: Insurance Institute for Applied Ethics, 1997).

Guideline G6.6 – Sound Judgment

Beyond the obligations under Rule R6.2, a CPCU should exercise caution and sound judgment in dealing with any confidential or privileged information.

R6.2 does not prohibit CPCUs from disclosing confidential information when it is required by law or when it is made to a person who must have the information in order to do his or her legitimate job. But that does not provide a license to share confidential information without first considering its implications. G6.6 encourages CPCUs to think before sharing sensitive information.

This Rule does not apply only to insurance-related information or activities. Although one might argue that complete privacy cannot necessarily be expected in some matters, the example below illustrates two ways in which information was certainly used beyond the intended purpose for which people had access.

Example

Bob, who works in information systems, has developed an amorous interest in Bonnie, a member of his CPCU 5 class who works in personnel. Bob monitors her e-mail to see whether she has other boyfriends or whether she says anything about him to her friends. Meanwhile, sensing his interest in her, Bonnie pulls his personnel file and checks his marital status, his income, and his performance review. Bob does not tell Bonnie he reads her e-mail, and Bonnie does not tell Bob she has checked his file.

Has a Rule been violated? Not only is such misuse of confidential information inappropriate, it might also be considered a violation of R6.2. In this case, confidential information entrusted to each candidate was disclosed to the candidates themselves for purposes other than legitimate occupational or professional duties.

What should Bob and Bonnie have done? They should strive to maintain a dignified and honorable relationship. Although this does not preclude a romantic relationship, sound judgment (indicated by G6.6) dictates that certain information, to which they have access for business reasons, should not be used for personal reasons.

Rule R6.3 – Acknowledging Limitations

In rendering or proposing to render professional services for others, a CPCU shall not knowingly misrepresent or conceal any limitations on the CPCU's ability to provide the quantity or quality of professional services required by the circumstances.

Guidelines

Guideline G6.1 – Exude Competence and Ethics

G6.1 First and foremost by exhibiting high levels of professional competence and ethical conduct, a CPCU should constantly strive to *merit* the confidence and respect of those whom they serve, fellow practitioners, and members of other professions.

The best way to obtain and maintain a good reputation is to earn it.

Guideline G6.2 and G6.3 – Relationships With Other Practitioners

Both G6.2 and G6.3 address relationships with other practitioners, and they will be examined together.

G6.2: A CPCU should strive to establish and maintain dignified and honorable relationships with competitors, as well as with other fellow practitioners.

G6.3 A CPCU should strive to establish and maintain dignified and honorable relationships with members of other professions, including but not limited to law, medicine, and accounting. The insurance industry relies heavily on the expertise and cooperation of such professionals in fulfilling its obligation to deliver insurance benefits promptly and otherwise render high quality insurance services to the public.

Relationships depend on all parties to the relationship, and striving to create and maintain a good relationship does not always ensure success. Nevertheless, CPCUs should strive to maintain good relationships not only with their counterparts in other professions, but also with their competitors and fellow practitioners—whether or not they are also CPCUs or CPCU candidates. This just makes good business sense.

In his essay, "The Evolution of Ethics in the CPCU Program,"[8] Frederick R. Hodosh tells the story of a long-time supporter of the American Institute who called the Institute president to complain about what he felt was a serious Code violation. The bottom line was that the young designee he was denouncing was "Just a smart aleck." Apparently this young CPCU had not succeeded in maintaining a dignified relationship with the old-timer, but being a "smart-aleck" does not, by itself, violate a Rule of the Code.

---

8. Frederick R. Hodosh, "The Evolution of Ethics in the CPCU Program," *Essays on Professionalism and Ethics* (Malvern, PA: Insurance Institute of America, 1998), p. 12.

The Ethics Counsel occasionally receives complaints regarding CPCUs who are not well-liked by their peers—because of their personality or for other reasons. An assertive personality that leads to business success is often considered abrasive by others. It is even true that some individual CPCUs are generally characterized by other CPCUs as "not a nice person." Popularity and respect do not necessarily go together. It is entirely possible to dislike someone as a person yet respect him or her as a professional. Dignified and honorable relationships among professionals are generally based on respect, if not popularity or friendship.

Guideline G6.4 – Independent Judgment

Like other professionals, a CPCU should maintain the knowledge and skills necessary to exercise independent judgment in the performance of his or her professional services. However, a CPCU should always be mindful of his or her personal limitations. A CPCU should not hesitate to seek the counsel of other professionals, therefore, not only at the request of those whom the CPCU may serve but also on the CPCU's own initiative, particularly in doubtful or difficult situations or when the quality of professional service may otherwise be enhanced by such consultation.

Guideline G6.4 adds another dimension to Rule R2.1, which requires CPCUs to keep informed on technical matters that relate to their area of practice. To live up to their aspirations as professionals, CPCUs should not only be informed. They should be informed well enough to exercise independent judgment. At the same time, in keeping with R6.1 and R6.3, they should recognize their legal and professional limitations. A CPCU should be willing to get advice from other professionals, both inside and outside the insurance/risk management profession. Not only should CPCUs be willing to seek outside advice; they should exercise the initiative to get it when it will enable them to better serve the public.

Independent judgment is an essential characteristic of many professionals. When we ask Dr. Smith, physician, for a second opinion, we do not expect to hear, "If that was Dr. Jones' opinion, then it must be right." When a Certified Public Accountant reviews a corporation's financial records, we do not expect to read, "Because this is what the corporation submitted, I believe it to be true." By the same token, any person passing professional judgment on an insurance or risk management situation ought to exercise independent judgment and also to acknowledge any limitations to his or her expertise in the matter, as well as any legal limitations.

Guideline G6.5 – Legal Limitations

A CPCU is obligated to keep fully informed on any and all legal limitations imposed upon the scope of his or her professional activities. A CPCU should always exercise caution to avoid engaging in, or giving the appearance of engaging in, the unauthorized practice of law. However, nothing herein should be construed as prohibiting the practice of law by a CPCU who is otherwise qualified by virtue of his or her admission to the bar.

It seems obvious that CPCUs who are not lawyers should not practice law, just as those who are not accountants should not practice accounting—and CPCUs who are not physicians should not attempt to perform surgery. But respecting legal limitations is more easily said than done. By their very nature, insurance and risk management practitioners deal constantly with legal relationships, legal rights, and other legal and contractual—and even medical—matters. CPCUs complete an entire course on business law, and much of their study in other areas is also based on an understanding of related legal principles. So it is quite common for CPCUs to be asked questions like, "Am I liable?" An authoritative answer to that question requires an attorney. CPCUs must often answer questions that are technically legal questions, and that is appropriate, so long as they do not presume to be authorities on the law. Some CPCUs, however, are also lawyers and are legally qualified to state an authoritative legal opinion.

CPCUs can easily be tempted to go beyond their authority. Because of their specialization in insurance, many CPCUs know more about certain insurance-related areas of the law than attorneys with other specialties who are authorized to render a legal opinion.

Related Code Provisions

Factors leading to dignified and honorable relationships are also mentioned in other parts of the Code:

- G6.4, suggesting that a professional should be able to exercise *independent* judgment, is closely related to R2.1, which requires a CPCU to keep informed on the technical matters necessary to remain professionally competent. Ideally, CPCUs should not only understand the issues; they should also understand them well enough to evaluate them and be able to express their own opinions.
- A violation of R3.3, requiring CPCUs not to violate any law or regulation relating to professional activities, can easily result from failure to keep informed of one's legal limitations, as required by R6.1.

- The Rules under Canon 8, especially those relating directly to the dignified use of the CPCU credential, are especially important in establishing dignified relationships with other professionals.

Relevant Hypothetical Case Studies

Hypothetical Case Studies appear later in this publication. The Rules under Canon 6 are considered in the following Hypothetical Case Studies:

- HCS 102
- HCS 103
- HCS 104
- HCS 110
- HCS 111
- HCS 117

Review Questions

Suggested answers appear elsewhere in this publication.

1. CPCUs should strive to establish and maintain dignified and honorable relationships with insurance practitioners and other professionals. What is the connection between professional relationships and ethical behavior?

2. A typical CPCU has devoted more attention to the study of insurance and related fields than most other insurance practitioners, and he or she should proudly display the CPCU designation and explain what it stands for. Yet, every CPCU has many limitations in his or her professional expertise. What steps should a CPCU take to compensate for these limitations?

3. Most insurance activities necessarily require the use of confidential business or personal information such as the specific injuries of an accident victim or the earnings of a firm's individual employees. Some items of information might even be relevant to civil or criminal actions. How is a CPCU supposed to treat confidential information while remaining true to both Canons 5 and 6?

Canon 7 – Public Education

CPCUs should assist in improving the public understanding of insurance and risk management.

CPCUs are among the most educated property-liability insurance practitioners. It is fitting for them to share their knowledge and understanding with the public in order to serve the public interest.

Rule R7.1 restates the broad goal in the Canon somewhat more narrowly. CPCUs are not obligated to directly provide public information, but they are ethically obligated to support efforts that get information to the public. Rule R7.2 provides the corollary—what CPCUs should not do. It certainly would not behoove CPCUs to use their knowledge and understanding to take advantage of a naïve public.

Because a public understanding of insurance and risk management can lead to improvements in the insurance mechanism, Canon 7 is closely related to part of Canon 4.

Rule R7.1 – Support Efforts to Provide Information

A CPCU shall support efforts to provide members of the public with objective information concerning their risk management and insurance needs and the products, services, and techniques which are available to meet their needs.

Rule R7.2 – Provide Accurate Information

A CPCU shall not misrepresent the benefits, costs, or limitations of any risk management technique or any product or service of an insurer.

Because Guideline G7.4 directly addresses Rule R7.2, it will be examined next.

Guideline G7.4 – Deceptive Advertising or Business Practice

A CPCU should neither engage in nor condone deceptive advertising or business practices which significantly mislead the public or otherwise contribute to the widespread misunderstanding or misuse of insurance. The minimum goal of all a CPCU's communications with the public should be to provide objective and factual information.

Other Guidelines

Guideline G7.1 – All CPCUs Should Improve Public Understanding

Fulfillment of all the public's insurance needs would appreciably enhance the economic and social well-being of society. But the public's insurance needs can be fully met only if every citizen recognizes his or her insurance needs and appreciates the importance of seeking competent and ethical assistance in analyzing and meeting these needs. The achievement of this result requires the combined efforts of all knowledgeable insurance professionals. Accordingly, every CPCU should assist in every practical manner to improve the public understanding of insurance and risk management even if the CPCU does not specialize in insurance education, marketing, claims settlement, safety engineering, advertising, or other professional activities which provide frequent opportunities to communicate directly to the public.

Some CPCUs work in positions that regularly involve writing for publication, public speaking, or other types of public contact. Most do not. CPCUs are not ethically required to enter into these activities. However, they are required to support them.

Though it might not be immediately obvious, CPCUs—even those who do not work in public relations, education, or other public-contact positions—have many opportunities to improve the public understanding of insurance and risk management. Here are just a few:

- Producers, claim representatives, and others who deal directly with the public should strive to explain insurance policies and transactions as clearly and completely as possible.
- Many CPCU chapters provide a speakers bureau service. Members are available to speak on insurance/risk management topics to outside groups. Scripts for some topics are provided by the CPCU Society.
- Many CPCU chapters support insurance education programs in local high schools and colleges. CPCUs can serve as adjunct faculty members, guest speakers, or committee members.
- Many CPCUs serve as course leaders for CPCU and IIA programs.
- CPCUs often serve as speakers and panelists for other professional organizations.
- CPCUs can make themselves available to members of the press who are looking for somebody to interview following a catastrophe or other newsworthy event. If someone knowledgeable is not readily available, often

the press will settle for the first apparent spokesperson, whether or not that person has any expertise.

- CPCU chapters engage in research projects.
- CPCUs, as individuals and in conjunction with others, write articles for the *CPCU Journal* and other publications. Some contribute to the public understanding by submitting letters to the editor in trade publications or community newspapers.

Guidelines G7.2 and G7.3 – Remain Current in Areas of Change

Because they are closely related, G7.2 and G7.3 will be discussed together.

G7.2 A CPCU should keep abreast of legislation, changing conditions and/ or other developments which may affect the insuring public, and should assist in keeping the public informed of such.

G7.3 In order to contribute to a better public understanding of insurance and risk management, it is essential for every CPCU to maintain and improve his or her own knowledge and communicative skills. However, no CPCU should hesitate to admit freely that he or she does not know the answer to a question. Nor should a CPCU attempt to answer such a question if it lies outside the realm of the CPCU's professional competence, authority, or proper function.

As noted in our discussion of Canon 2 and its only rule, Rule R2.1, CPCUs are ethically obligated to keep current, at least in the areas required to do their jobs. They are required by R4.2 to support improvements in the insurance mechanism. G6.4 points out that CPCUs should understand the issues well enough to exercise independent judgment. G7.2 indicates that CPCUs should also aspire to keep abreast of changes that might affect the public so that they can help explain these changes to the public. Now, G7.3 amplifies the entire discussion by pointing out that knowledge is of limited use unless it can be communicated.

CPCU candidates are held to the same rules as CPCUs. Both candidates and CPCUs should not hesitate to admit that they do not know the answer to a question, nor should they attempt to answer a question they cannot competently address. This is a Guideline, not a Rule, and it is intended for use in practical situations. We might mention, tongue-in-cheek, that candidates should not follow this advice when taking a CPCU national exam where there is no penalty for guessing. But seriously, developing the communication skills necessary to compose the answers to essay-type CPCU exams does enable

CPCU candidates to develop the communication skills necessary to promote a public understanding of insurance and risk management.

Guideline G7.5 – Limitations of Insurance

It is highly desirable for the public to recognize its overall risk management needs and the limitations and advantages of insurance in meeting such needs. For instance, a CPCU should seize every opportunity to stress the importance of loss prevention and reduction in any well-conceived risk management program.

This Guideline is addressed to the many CPCUs who work directly for insurance companies or related organizations. Insurance is not the only answer, the best answer, or even an appropriate answer for addressing some risk management needs. Given their broad educational background, all CPCUs should recognize that loss control measures and alternative risk financing measures (other than insurance) are appropriate and desirable components of many risk management programs.

The Code was conceived at a time when many insurance practitioners believed "risk management" was a competitor of insurance. Today's enlightened professionals recognize that every job is most effectively handled when the right tools are used, and insurance is only one of several risk management tools.

It is sometimes said that when the only tool you have is a hammer, then everything looks like a nail. It can be difficult for insurance producers and others—whose main tool is insurance—to recognize that some situations are best handled without insurance. But professionals have a responsibility to recommend the most appropriate tool, not only the one that is part of their portfolio.

Guideline G7.6 – Objective Public Information

Rule R7.1 stipulates that "A CPCU shall support efforts to provide members of the public with objective information concerning their risk management and insurance needs and the products, services, and techniques which are available to meet their needs." Both in the *Rules* and in the *Guidelines* above, the needs referred to are those which exist (at a point in time, understood) and the products, services, and techniques referred to are those which are available (at a point in time, understood). Neither the *Rules* nor the *Guidelines* require a CPCU to support lobbying efforts or proposed legislation, or the taking of positions on controversial issues. Nor do any of the *Code* standards prohibit a CPCU from engaging in such activities, in his

or her own name and as an individual. However, a CPCU who elects to engage in such activities should take great care to avoid violating Rule R8.4.

G7.6 answers a question that has not directly been posed. The gist of the question is this: "If CPCUs are ethically obligated to provide objective public information on insurance-related products that meet the public's needs, does it follow that CPCUs are ethically obligated to support legislation that would provide new insurance products?" The complete question is even more complicated, but that paraphrase will do for purposes of this discussion.

The answer to this unexpressed question is that CPCUs are expected to deal with the world as it is, not as it ought to be. That is the point of the parenthetical additions, "(at a point in time, understood)." The point is that CPCUs are ethically obligated to deal with *current* needs and *current* services that address those needs, as well as with expected changes. CPCUs are not ethically required to lobby or otherwise inform the public of services that *might* become available *if* certain legislation is passed. In fact, G7.6 explicitly states that CPCUs are not ethically required to take positions on pending legislation or other controversial issues. However, they should exercise independent judgment and continually study the issues.

Although CPCUs are not required to be politically active, they are not prohibited either. Rule R4.2 might even require taking a position on some issues that would improve the insurance mechanism. And when taking a position, it is appropriate to identify oneself as a CPCU. The CPCU designation says something about where one is "coming from." A CPCU designation indicates that the holder has met a certain standard involving education, experience, and ethics and has a firm foundation for expressing a professional opinion. At the same time, a single CPCU cannot express the views of all CPCUs. Neither can a single CPCU represent the views of the American Institute for CPCU—unless, of course, he or she is authorized by the Institute to do so.

The Code of Professional Ethics of the American Institute prohibits CPCUs from appearing to represent the Institute. CPCUs who are members of the CPCU Society are also subject to the CPCU Society's Code of Ethics, which includes the following "specified unethical practice":

> To write, speak, or act in such a way as to lead another to reasonably believe that the member is officially representing the Society or a chapter of the Society unless the member has been duly authorized to do so.

The CPCU Society, not the American Institute, is responsible for enforcing the CPCU Society's Code of Ethics.

Related Code Provisions

Other portions of the Code also relate to CPCUs' activities in promoting a public understanding of insurance and risk management:

- Canon 2 and R2.1 indicate the importance of continuous learning to understand the issues.

- R4.2 requires CPCUs to support efforts to improve the insurance mechanism; doing so often involves public education.

- R5.3 requires CPCUs to support certain types of laws and regulations that will benefit the public. As with R4.2, this often requires public education.

- While it is appropriate, and even desirable, for CPCUs to give visibility to their designation when speaking or writing publicly, R8.4 cautions CPCUs to avoid leaving any appearance that a CPCU is speaking on behalf of the American Institute.

Relevant Hypothetical Case Studies

Hypothetical Case Studies appear elsewhere in this publication. Four published Hypothetical Case Studies include mention of Canon 7 or the rules that relate to it:

- HCS 106
- HCS 107
- HCS 109
- HCS 111

Review Question

Suggested answers appear elsewhere in this publication.

1. One way of improving the insurance mechanism is to support proposed legislation that a CPCU believes is favorable and consistent with the goals of service to the public. Does the Code encourage or discourage lobbying efforts by a CPCU speaking as an individual?

2. What precautions should a CPCU take when expressing a position on political issues or other issues?

Canon 8 – Integrity of the CPCU Designation

CPCUs should honor the integrity of the CPCU designation and respect the limitations placed on its use.

We often speak of a person, or even an organization, as having **integrity**. However, "integrity" might seem like an unusual attribute to apply to the CPCU designation. According to Webster's New World Dictionary, the word has three meanings:

1. The quality or state of being complete; unbroken condition; wholeness; entirety
2. The quality or state of being unimpaired; perfect condition; soundness
3. The quality or state of being of sound moral principle; uprightness, honesty, and sincerity[9]

Honoring the integrity of the CPCU designation means doing one's best to ensure the well-being of this hard-earned professional designation, thus doing everything possible to preserve its sound reputation.

The Rules under this Canon take several different directions. The integrity of the CPCU professional designation is honored when the designation, and the key that symbolizes it, are used in a professional, dignified manner. Rule R8.1 and the related Guidelines (which are part of the Rule) are explicit in specifying the ways in which the designation and key should be used.

The Rules and Guidelines associated with Canon 8 attempt to achieve a delicate balance between two issues: visibility and dignity. CPCUs are encouraged to display and use their designation proudly in order to enhance the recognition of this professional credential in the eyes of the public. At the same time, CPCUs are required to use the designation and the key in ways that preserve the professional dignity that has always been associated with the CPCU movement.

While giving high visibility to the CPCU designation, CPCUs should not overstate its significance or unfairly imply that people who are not CPCUs are inferior. Many qualified and well-educated insurance professionals do not hold the CPCU designation.

Another "limitation": CPCUs should not imply that holding the CPCU designation empowers them to speak as representatives of the American Institute,

---

9. *Webster's New World Dictionary Third College Edition*, s.v. "integrity."

which granted the designation. Few questions have come up concerning this Rule, and perhaps it is fairly obvious.

Rule R8.1 – Use of the CPCU Designation and Key

A CPCU shall use the CPCU designation and the CPCU key only in accordance with the relevant *Guidelines* promulgated by the American Institute.

This is the only Rule in the entire Code that specifically refers to the Guidelines, and this reference has an important effect. The Guidelines that appear in the originally published Code, as well as in the form of published advisory opinions, are a part of this Rule, and failure to adhere to these Guidelines is a Rule violation.

The relevant Guideline is G8.1, which will be discussed immediately. Because of its length, some comments are sandwiched between portions of the Guideline.

Guideline G8.1 – Authorized Uses of the CPCU Key and Designation

Rule R8.1 of the *Code of Professional Ethics* stipulates that "A CPCU shall use the CPCU designation and the CPCU key only in accordance with the relevant *Guidelines* promulgated by the American Institute." These *Guidelines*, which define and impose restrictions upon the privilege to use the CPCU designation and key, are set forth below. They are designed to prevent undignified commercialization of the designation, unfair comparisons with able and well-established insurance practitioners who do not hold the designation, and other unethical practices which are inconsistent with the professional concepts which CPCU represents. Specifically, every CPCU has an ethical obligation to comply with the following minimum standards:

"Dignified and professional" are important words in the explanation that follows. There can be differences of opinion as to what is dignified and professional. The Institute generally applies a fairly conservative standard. As noted later, any use besides those specifically authorized below must first be approved by the American Institute. When in doubt, CPCUs are urged to request appropriate permission.

   a. **The designation Chartered Property Casualty Underwriter, the initials CPCU, and the CPCU key may be used only in a dignified and professional manner.**

   1. **The designation or initials may be used after the holder's name on business cards, stationery, office advertising, signed articles,**

business and professional listings, and telephone listings, except where such use would conflict with the provisions of subparagraph a.3. below.

2. The CPCU key (actual size or reduced, but not enlarged) may be imprinted only on business cards and stationery used exclusively by CPCUs. Copies of the CPCU key suitable for reproduction are available from the American Institute.

3. The CPCU designation being personal in nature, the designation itself, the initials CPCU, and the CPCU key are not to be used as part of a firm, partnership, or corporate name, trademark, or logo, or affixed to any object, product, property, for any purpose whatsoever, except by the American Institute.

What is the "actual size" of the CPCU key? As explained below, camera-ready copies of the key are made available to designees and CPCUs wishing to use it as approved. The actual-size key is $1^1/4''$ high, and reproductions larger than that are not permitted on business cards and stationery.

Because the CPCU designation is rightfully associated only with the person who has earned it, it may not appropriately be used as part of a business name or logo.

The second part of provision 3 is especially important: Except as specifically authorized in provisions 1 and 2, the CPCU initials (whether upper-case or lower-case), and the CPCU key, are *not* to be affixed to any object except by the American Institute or, as noted later, with the explicit permission of the Institute.

b. The designation Chartered Property Casualty Underwriter, the initials CPCU, and the CPCU key may be used to announce the conferment of the designation.

1. News releases prepared by the American Institute are mailed to all new CPCU designees. Only these approved releases, with the addition of personal biographical information, may be used by individual CPCU designees in preparing material for the business and community press.

Approved news releases are carefully worded to give due visibility to the accomplishment of the designee, while preserving the dignity of the CPCU designation, and to avoid any wording that might violate R8.2 or R8.3.

2. The American Institute encourages employers of new designees to publish in company publications articles congratulating the new designees. The American Institute's official listing of new

designees, published at the time of the conferment ceremony, should be used to verify the names of new designees. Copies of the CPCU key are available from the American Institute for reproduction in such articles.

3. The American Institute encourages the appearance of dignified advertisements congratulating new designees on earning the CPCU designation. Copies of the CPCU key are available from the American Institute for reproduction in such advertisements. These advertisements must be strictly congratulatory in nature, however, and should not include the business conducted by the firm, the lines of insurance carried by the firm, the firm's telephone number, or any copy soliciting business.

c. The designation Chartered Property Casualty Underwriter, the initials CPCU, and the CPCU key may be used by the CPCU Society in a manner which complies with the *Rules* and *Guidelines* of the American Institute's *Code of Professional Ethics*, and which has first been authorized in writing by the Ethics Counsel of the American Institute.

The CPCU Society sells CPCU jewelry and other items bearing the CPCU designation and/or key. Items sold by the Society have been approved by the American Institute, unless they reflect the CPCU Society logo rather than the CPCU letters or key.

d. The designation Chartered Property Casualty Underwriter, the initials CPCU, and the CPCU key may not be used in any manner which violates a *Rule* of the *Code of Professional Ethics*. *Rules R8.2, R8.3, and R8.4* deserve special mention in this context since they relate directly to, and impose restrictions upon, the privilege to use the CPCU designation.

e. The designation Chartered Property Casualty Underwriter, the initials CPCU, and the CPCU key may be used in any other manner which has received prior approval in writing from the Ethics Counsel of the American Institute.

The American Institute responds promptly to such requests. Use of the CPCU designation on custom-made items of jewelry or other objects is not authorized unless it is specifically approved by the Ethics Counsel. Before requesting permission, CPCUs should be sure that the requested use meets high standards of dignity and professionalism. Because the designation is personal in nature, CPCUs should also ensure that the object bearing the key or designation will be associated only with a CPCU. For example, a jewelry pin that reads: "My Mommy's a CPCU" could not be approved.

f. Any questions regarding the interpretation of these *Guidelines* should be directed to the American Institute's Board of Ethical Inquiry. A prompt response will be made to all such requests.

This Guideline has been supplemented by two published Advisory Opinions. The first prohibits the use of the "CPCU" letters, by themselves or along with other letters or numbers, on auto license plates. A second Guideline, published in 1998, appears under the following heading. As noted earlier, Rule R8.1 incorporates by reference any guidelines published by the Institute, and these Advisory Opinions therefore have the force of a Rule. Usage prohibited by these Advisory Opinions could lead to sanctions under the enforcement provisions of the Code.

1998 Advisory Opinion – Internet Use and Telephone Listings

In response to several recent inquiries, the Board of Ethical Inquiry (BEI) has issued the following Advisory Opinion regarding the appropriate use of the CPCU designation and key on World Wide Web pages of the Internet. For obvious reasons, these uses were not contemplated when the Code was drafted in the 1970s.

The BEI also addressed the related question of whether the letters "CPCU" could appropriately be used as part of an Internet home page or e-mail address. The BEI also thought it appropriate at this time to promulgate a specific opinion regarding the use of the letters "CPCU" as part of an advertised telephone number. Several years ago, the BEI issued an Advisory Opinion prohibiting the use of the letters "CPCU" alone or with other letters or numbers on an automobile vanity license plate.

This Advisory Opinion is a specific interpretation of the provisions of the Code of Professional Ethics of the American Institute.

Advisory Opinion Regarding Use of the Designation Chartered Property Casualty Underwriter, the Initials CPCU, and the CPCU Key on a Web Page

The Guidelines applicable to business cards, stationery, office advertising, signed articles, business and professional listings, and telephone listings also apply to usage on Web pages by CPCUs or organizations employing CPCUs. Among other things, CPCU keys should not be enlarged, the designation should relate only to individual designation-holders (not the firm), and any explanation should not directly or indirectly overstate the value of the designation. All usage should be professional and dignified in nature. CPCUs are encouraged, at their option, to link their Web pages to the American Institute's Web page at www.aicpcu.org. (The CPCU Society also encourages members to link to its Web page at www.cpcusociety.org.)

The American Institute for CPCU, the CPCU Society, and CPCU Society chapters may use the designation Chartered Property Casualty Underwriter, the initials CPCU, and the CPCU key on a Web page, where they may also use the designation or initials as part of the organization name, provided the usage is otherwise consistent with these guidelines.

Any questions regarding the appropriateness of existing or draft Web pages may be directed to the Ethics Counsel of the American Institute.

Advisory Opinion Regarding Use of the Initials CPCU in a Web Page or E-mail Address

The initials CPCU, whether upper or lower case, by themselves or within a longer address, may not be used as part of a Web page or e-mail address, except by the American Institute for CPCU, the CPCU Society, and CPCU Society chapters.

Any individuals or businesses that currently use "cpcu" as part of a Web or e-mail address should contact their Internet service provider and change the address before January 1, 1999.

Advisory Opinion Regarding Use of the Initials CPCU in a Telephone Number

The initials CPCU, whether upper or lower case, should not be used as part of a telephone "number" in advertisements, publications, or other listings except by the American Institute for CPCU, the CPCU Society, and CPCU Society chapters.

As soon as practicable, any listings that currently use the letters "CPCU" should instead use the related numbers "2728."

Rule R8.2 – Overstating CPCU

A CPCU shall not attribute to the mere possession of the designation depth or scope of knowledge, skills, and professional capabilities greater than those demonstrated by successful completion of the CPCU program.

Guideline G8.2, which follows immediately, elaborates on the intent of this Rule.

Guideline G8.2 – Misrepresentation

Rule R8.2 stipulates that "A CPCU shall not attribute to the *mere possession of the designation* [emphasis supplied] depth or scope of knowledge, skills, and professional capabilities greater than those demonstrated by successful completion of the CPCU program." Unless this *Rule* is strictly observed by all CPCUs, the public will be misled and the integrity of the designation, as well as the integrity of the violator, will be significantly diminished.

CPCUs can be justifiably proud of having passed the rigorous qualifying exams and of having met the ethical and experience requirements imposed by the American Institute. But the CPCU curriculum, comprehensive though it is, does not in itself make a person an expert in every insurance and insurance-related area. Moreover, the CPCU curriculum has been periodically altered over the years to accommodate revised educational needs and objectives.

Consider, for instance, the case of an agent whose CPCU designation was conferred in a year prior to 1978. Such an agent would clearly violate R8.2 if he or she led a prospective client to believe that the possession of the CPCU designation made him or her a qualified expert in life, health, or group insurance, particularly since the curriculum at that time provided little or no study or testing in these areas. The agent might otherwise have become a qualified expert in life, health, or group insurance, perhaps through experience and/or other formal educational programs, but it would be unethical to attribute this expertise to his or her possession of the CPCU designation per se. In short, the public is protected and the integrity of the designation and its holder are best preserved by avoiding any misrepresentations of the nature and significance of the CPCU designation.

Rule R8.3 – Comparison With Non-CPCUs

A CPCU shall not make unfair comparisons between a person who holds the CPCU designation and one who does not.

Rule R8.4 – Acting as a Representative of the American Institute

A CPCU shall not write, speak, or act in such a way as to lead another to reasonably believe the CPCU is officially representing the American Institute, unless the CPCU has been duly authorized to do so by the American Institute.

The vast majority of CPCUs are not official representatives of the American Institute, and they should not imply that they speak for the Institute. Normally, the only people who have the authority to speak on behalf of the Institute are the officers and staff of the Institute, as well as members of the American Institute's Board of Trustees. Since many Institute employees and trustees are CPCUs, it was necessary to add the "unless" line to the Rule.

The issue of "acting as a representative of the Institute" could arise in connection with local CPCU conferment ceremonies. Most CPCU chapters conduct an annual graduation ceremony in which they honor the current year's CPCU designees, following procedures specifically established by the American Institute. These procedures specify who is entitled to act as a representative of the Institute in conducting these local ceremonies, and the American Institute works with the CPCU Society in making sure an appropriate representative is available.

The Code of Professional Ethics of the American Institute includes Rules that the Institute's graduates and students must follow to avoid sanctions under the Code; the Code of Professional Ethics of the American Institute for CPCU is not the appropriate place to address standards of conduct for CPCU Society members in their role as members. Neither R8.2 nor anything else in the Code addresses whether it is appropriate for CPCUs to speak on behalf of the CPCU Society. These issues are addressed in the CPCU Society's Code of Ethics, which appears later in this publication. Moreover, common sense indicates that ordinary members do not have the authority to speak on behalf of their organization as a whole, and doing so might involve deceit, in violation of Rule R3.1.

Other Related Code Provisions

- Most other Code provisions allude to situations in which CPCUs use their designation as a credential, to enhance their credibility and to give visibility to the CPCU movement, whether dealing with customers, the general public, or other insurance and noninsurance professionals. It is not necessary to elaborate on this point.

- While R8.1 deals with the appropriate use of the designation, Rule R9.3 addresses *unauthorized* use of the CPCU designation by an individual who is not a CPCU. CPCUs are ethically obligated to report such incidents.

Relevant Hypothetical Case Studies

Hypothetical Case Studies appear elsewhere in this publication. Only one Hypothetical Case Study, HCS 120, involves issues relating directly to Canon 8.

Review Questions

Suggested answers appear elsewhere in this publication.

1. How might Rule R8.4 be violated by a CPCU who is engaged in lobbying efforts?

2. In what ways does Canon 8 seek to maintain the dignity of the CPCU professional designation?

3. The Code includes specific restrictions on the ways in which the CPCU designation and the CPCU key are to be used:

    (a) What problems are these restrictions designed to prevent?

    (b) List the specific ways described in the Code in which the initials CPCU and the CPCU key may be used.

    (c) List the specific prohibitions against misuse of the CPCU designation or the CPCU key.

4. What are appropriate ways of announcing that a CPCU candidate has met all requirements and has earned and received the CPCU professional designation?

Canon 9 – Integrity of the Code

CPCUs should assist in maintaining the integrity of the *Code of Professional Ethics*.

Both Canon 8 and 9 deal with integrity. While Canon 8 deals with the integrity of the CPCU designation, Canon 9 deals with the integrity of the Code of Professional Ethics. Like any code of ethics, the Code of Professional Ethics has integrity only if those who are bound by it consider it important and adhere to it. To maintain its integrity, the Code must also be enforced, and sanctions must be imposed on those who violate the Rules of the Code.

How can CPCUs assist in maintaining the integrity of the Code? That is addressed in the Rules following Canon 9. CPCUs support the Code's integrity by supporting only candidates who meet the ethical standards of the Code and by assisting the Institute in enforcing the Code. CPCUs are also *required* to report any use of the CPCU designation by someone who is not authorized to do so.

Rule R9.1 – Supporting Candidates Who Meet Ethical Standards

A CPCU shall not initiate or support the CPCU candidacy of any individual known by the CPCU to engage in business practices which violate the ethical standards prescribed by this Code.

This Rule stands as a complement to Rule R5.2: "A CPCU shall encourage and assist qualified individuals who wish to pursue CPCU. . . ." While encouraging qualified individuals, CPCUs should neither initiate nor support the candidacy of any individual who engages in unethical business practices. What business practices are unethical? Those that violate the standards of the Code.

Note that R9.1 refers not to the Rules of the Code, but rather to "the ethical standards prescribed by this Code." CPCUs are to initiate and support only those CPCU candidates with the high ethical standards reflected not only in the Rules, but also in the Canons.

Example

The CPCU Society and the American Institute for CPCU jointly administer a Personal Sponsorship Program under which CPCUs are matched with CPCU or IIA candidates to serve as mentors. Karen Brown, CPCU, signed up to become a personal sponsor and was matched with Claude Baker, a CPCU candidate. During the next two years, as she encourages Claude and helps with his studies, she also gets to know him better and, in the process, discovers some things about his personality and attitude that disturb her. Specifically, Claude seems more interested in manipulating people to make a buck than in performing his job with diligence and serving the best interests of his customers.

Has a Rule been violated by Claude or Karen? Having been a CPCU student for several years, Claude is presumably a matriculated candidate subject to the Code. Karen apparently senses that Claude does not aspire to the high standards of Canon 1, Canon 3, Canon 4, and possibly other Canons.

The question of a Rule violation by Claude could be answered by the BEI only if it were presented with specific, documented evidence in a formal complaint.

It would take much more information to determine whether Karen would violate Rule R9.1 by continuing to support Claude's candidacy. Based on the information here, it seems that her continued support at least violates her sound professional judgment.

What should Karen do? We'll assume that Karen has shared her concerns with Claude and attempted, unsuccessfully, to get him to change his attitude. At this point, it would be appropriate for Karen to contact her local CPCU chapter, the CPCU Society, and the American Institute and formally withdraw her sponsorship of Claude. Karen should recognize, however, that withdrawing her sponsorship will not affect Claude's status as a CPCU candidate. If she has specific evidence of a Rule violation, she is not required to report it (see R9.2 and G9.2), but she might choose to file a formal ethics complaint against him. Depending on the outcome of its investigation, the BEI might suspend Claude's candidacy for a Rule violation, but not merely for losing the support of his sponsor.

In any case, Karen should not be concerned that withdrawing her support works against the best interests of the CPCU movement. Although growth in the number of CPCUs is important, the quality of those who hold the designation is even more important (see Guideline G9.1, below).

Because Guideline G9.1 relates most directly to Rule R9.1, it is discussed next, before the other rules are examined.

Guideline G9.1 – Maintaining Standards

It is not an objective of the American Institute to achieve growth in the number of CPCUs at the expense of professional standards, but rather to encourage more qualified individuals to meet the high standards which have always characterized the CPCU designation requirements. A CPCU should assist in upholding the experience, educational, and ethical

standards prescribed for prospective CPCU designees by the American Institute for Chartered Property Casualty Underwriters.

Taken together with Rule R9.1, this Guideline serves as a reminder that the goal is not strictly to increase the number of CPCUs, at least not if it means sacrificing standards. The CPCU movement is founded on the goal of raising professional standards in property and liability insurance. This goal would not be met if standards were lowered in order to increase the number of CPCUs, CPCU candidates, or CPCU exam passers.

G9.1 relates not only to standards for candidates, but also to support for the standards of the American Institute. The CPCU movement is best served when CPCUs, who have completed the program, continue to support high standards for present and future candidates—even if lowered standards would increase the number of future CPCU completers.

The American Institute is challenged to provide an appropriate curriculum, quality textbooks, fair exams, and study materials that assist candidates in meeting educational objectives so that they can pass the exams. At the same time, the American Institute is challenged by the need to inform thousands of students each year that they have not yet demonstrated that they have met the high standards required to pass a CPCU exam. Some are unable to meet the standards and will not—and should not—become CPCUs. Others are challenged to try again in order to prove that they can meet those standards.

Achieving growth in the number of CPCUs while maintaining high standards presents challenges similar to those that insurance companies face when they plan to increase premium volume while maintaining a favorable loss ratio. But while insurance companies face competition from other insurers who provide similar services, only the American Institute can award the CPCU designation, a designation that has earned its reputation as the premiere credential in property and liability insurance. While CPCU is not for everyone, there is a large pool of insurance and risk management practitioners who would make good CPCUs, and all CPCUs should identify them, recruit them as CPCU candidates, and encourage and support their candidacy.

Rule R9.2 – Reporting Violations

A CPCU possessing unprivileged information concerning an alleged violation of this Code shall, upon request, reveal such information to the tribunal or other authority empowered by the American Institute to investigate or act upon the alleged violation.

Guidelines G9.2 and G9.3 relate primarily to this Rule and will be discussed next.

Guideline G9.2 – Reporting Adverse Information

A CPCU should assist the American Institute in preserving the integrity of the *Code of Professional Ethics*, first and foremost by voluntarily complying with both the letter and the spirit of the *Code*. Ultimately, however, the public can be protected and the integrity of the *Code* can be maintained only if the *Code* is strictly but fairly enforced, and this, in turn, can be achieved only if *Code* violations are promptly brought to the attention of the proper officials. Although a CPCU should not become a self-appointed investigator or judge on matters properly left to the Board of Ethical Inquiry, every CPCU should comply with the mandates of *Rules R9.1, R9.2,* and *R9.3. Except* for the comparatively rare but troublesome situation covered by *R9.3*, whether a CPCU should *volunteer* adverse information is left to the judgment of the CPCU.

Some professions have ethics rules that effectively prohibit one member from criticizing another member of the profession. The authors of the Code believed such provisions are contrary to the public interest. Indeed, the authors wrestled with the difficult question of whether CPCUs should be ethically obligated to report the misconduct of another CPCU. The ethics code in medicine obligates a physician to expose, without hesitation, the illegal or unethical conduct of another physician. The CPCU Code does not go quite that far. It forbids a CPCU from initiating or supporting the CPCU candidacy of a person known to engage in practices which violate the Code. It obligates a CPCU to furnish information when officially requested to do so by the proper Institute ethics authority. And it obligates a CPCU to report promptly to the Institute the use of the CPCU designation by an unauthorized person.

CPCUs are encouraged to report Code violations so the Code can be enforced and its integrity maintained. CPCUs sometimes ask whether they are ethically *required* to report a Code violation by another CPCU or CPCU candidate. None of the Rules requires CPCUs to "squeal" on other CPCUs. G9.2 makes it quite clear that it is up to CPCUs' judgment whether to report on another CPCU. Remember, though, that a CPCU would violate R1.2 if he or she advocates, sanctions, participates in, or even condones a Rule violation by another CPCU—or even by someone who is not a CPCU. CPCUs should also recognize that they can best preserve the integrity of their code of ethics by taking steps that will lead to sanctions against those who violate it.

In short, Canon 9 should inspire CPCUs to report Code violations, but no Rule specifically requires it. However, in deciding not to report another CPCU's violations, a CPCU should be sure he or she does not violate R1.2 by condoning the violation.

Guideline G9.3 – Committee Service

Upon request, a CPCU should serve on such committees, boards, or tribunals as are prescribed by the Institute for the administration or enforcement of the *Code*. A CPCU is obligated to disqualify himself or herself from such service (i) if the CPCU believes, in good conscience, that he or she could not serve in a fair and impartial manner or (ii) upon request.

This Guideline speaks for itself. The American Institute has never had a problem in recruiting CPCUs to serve on the Board of Ethical Inquiry or the Ethics Policy Committee of the Board of Trustees. At the same time, a CPCU who serves in such a role should disengage himself or herself from matters in which he or she has a personal interest, or in any other case where professional judgment suggests that he or she could not be objective.

Rule R9.3 – Reporting Unauthorized Use of the Designation

A CPCU shall report promptly to the American Institute any information concerning the use of the CPCU designation by an unauthorized person.

CPCUs are *ethically required* under the Code to report any use of the CPCU designation by someone who is not entitled to do so.

Only CPCUs and matriculated CPCU candidates are bound by the Code of Professional Ethics and subject to its sanctions. Persons who do not fall into these categories cannot be sanctioned by the Board of Ethical Inquiry. They can, however, violate the law in misappropriating the CPCU® designation, which has been trademarked by the American Institute for CPCU. The Institute's General Counsel will vigorously enforce the Institute's trademark rights under civil law.

CPCU candidates who use the CPCU designation before they are entitled to do so, or without meeting all requirements of the CPCU program, may be sanctioned under the Code. Penalties may include suspending their rights to complete the program.

CPCU candidates who have taken all necessary exams are not authorized to use the CPCU designation until the date they are specifically authorized by the American Institute to do so.

Until they officially become CPCUs, CPCU candidates are not to wear the CPCU key or other CPCU jewelry, use the CPCU designation after their name, or use business cards or stationery bearing the designation. It is appropriate, however, to order CPCU jewelry and stationery so that it is available for use as soon as it becomes appropriate.

Other Related Code Provisions

- R5.2 requires CPCUs to encourage and assist *qualified* individuals in pursuing CPCU studies, while R9.1 makes it abundantly clear that CPCUs should not support candidates whose business practices violate the Code's ethical standards.

- R6.2 requires CPCUs not to disclose confidential information unless it is required by law or made to a person who must have the information in order to discharge "legitimate occupational or professional duties." G9.2 makes it clear that reporting code violations is encouraged but not mandatory, to preserve the integrity of the Code. Enforcing the Code is a "legitimate professional duty."

Relevant Hypothetical Case Studies

Hypothetical Case Studies appear elsewhere in this publication. Two Hypothetical Case Studies involve Canon 9 and related Rules:

- HCS 101
- HCS 104

Review Questions

Suggested answers appear elsewhere in this publication.

1. Under what circumstances should a CPCU reveal information regarding a Code violator?
2. Is a CPCU obligated to report a non-CPCU who uses the CPCU designation?

The Canons, Rules, and Guidelines of the Code of Professional Ethics

Canon 1

CPCUs should endeavor at all times to place the public interest above their own.

Rules of Professional Conduct

R1.1   A CPCU has a duty to understand and abide by all *Rules* of conduct which are prescribed in the *Code of Professional Ethics* of the American Institute.

R1.2   A CPCU shall not advocate, sanction, participate in, cause to be accomplished, otherwise carry out through another, or condone any act which the CPCU is prohibited from performing by the *Rules* of this *Code*.

Guidelines for Professional Conduct

G1.1   By stipulating at the outset that "CPCUs Should Endeavor at All Times to Place the Public Interest Above Their Own," *Canon 1* serves as the fundamental goal of the entire *Code of Professional Ethics*. The other Code Standards are essentially attempts to define the "public interest" (and hence the ethical obligations of CPCUs) in more specific terms. Accordingly, the format of the *Code* is best understood by reading *Canon 1*, asking the question, "how?" and then reading the first two *Rules*. That is to say, how do CPCUs go about endeavoring at all times to place the public interest above their own? Answer: at a minimum, by understanding and obeying all the *Rules* in the *Code* (as specified in *R1.1* and *R1.2*) and then, beyond the expected minimums, by striving to meet the more lofty standards expressed in the *Canons* and the *Guidelines*.

The aspirational goal of *Canon 1* is more easily expressed than achieved. Indeed, one doubts whether any profession can ultimately make good the claim that all of its practitioners are forever guided by an attitude of altruism and a spirit of unselfish devotion to the needs of others. Nonetheless, a formal commitment to altruism is probably the single most important characteristic which distinguishes professional from unprofessional behavior.

G1.2   In the performance of his or her professional services, a CPCU should avoid even the appearance of impropriety and should generally act each day in a manner that will best serve the CPCU's own professional interests in the long run. This *Guideline*, when taken along with the other provisions of the *Code*, should pose no insurmountable problems of priority in the context of most everyday situations, since the best long-term professional interests of a CPCU ordinarily do not conflict either with the public interest or with other specific interests. However, it should be acknowledged that potential conflicts of interest may arise, or may appear to arise, because many CPCUs simultaneously serve two or more "masters," and they must somehow balance the various interests with their own personal interests and the best interests of the general public. For example, a CPCU who is employed by an insurance company may serve his or her immediate superior, the corporation, the stockholders, the policyholders, agents, and industry associations. An agent may serve his or her clients, two or more insurers, and his or her business partners, stockholders, or associates.

Strict compliance with all the *Rules* of this *Code*, including *R1.2*, should enable a CPCU to resolve such potential conflicts of interest which may arise. However, when there is good reason for a person subject to the Code to be uncertain as to the ethical propriety of a specific activity or type of conduct, that person should refrain from engaging in such activity or conduct until the matter has been clarified. Any CPCU or CPCU candidate who needs assistance in interpreting the *Code* is encouraged to request an advisory opinion from the American Institute's Board of Ethical Inquiry.

G1.3   The ethical obligation to place the public interest above personal interests or financial gain extends to every CPCU, regardless of whether or not the CPCU's occupational position requires direct contact with actual or prospective insurance consumers.

G1.4   Nothing in these *Guidelines* should be interpreted to mean that insurance purchasers should be given priority over deserving insurance claimants since the needs and best interests of insurance purchasers are in fact served only when all deserving insurance claimants, including third-party liability claimants, are accorded prompt, equitable, and otherwise fair treatment.

Canon 2

CPCUs should seek continually to maintain and improve their professional knowledge, skills, and competence.

Rules of Professional Conduct

R2.1   A CPCU shall keep informed on those technical matters that are essential to the maintenance of the CPCU's professional competence in insurance, risk management, or related fields.

Guidelines for Professional Conduct

G2.1   Though knowledge and skills alone do not ensure that an individual will adhere to high ethical standards, knowledge and skills are requisites to the high levels of competence and performance rightfully expected of all professionals. Indeed, to the extent that an individual purports to be a professional and yet does not maintain high levels of competence and performance, that individual engages in unethical conduct which is in the nature of a misrepresentation.

In order to earn the CPCU designation, every CPCU candidate demonstrated a mastery of insurance and related subjects by successfully completing a series of rigorous qualifying examinations of the American Institute for Chartered Property Casualty Underwriters. However, for any individual to maintain and improve the knowledge and skills which are requisites to high levels of competence and performance, it is essential for that individual to continue studying throughout his or her working life. This is especially true for practitioners in a business like insurance, which is characterized not only by its existing complexities but also by rapid changes in the business and in the legal, economic, and social environments within which it operates.

In recognition of the foregoing, each and every CPCU has an *ethical* obligation to engage actively and continuously in appropriate educational activities.

G2.2   At a *minimum*, as specified in *Rule R2.1*, "A CPCU shall keep informed on those technical matters that are essential to the maintenance of the CPCU's professional competence in insurance, risk management, or related fields." Since CPCUs serve as agents, brokers, underwriters, claims representatives, actuaries, risk managers, regulators, company executives, and specialists in a wide variety of insurance-related fields, the *Rule* does not attempt to prescribe the specific technical matters that are essential to the maintenance of professional competence in each of the numerous specialties. Instead, it is left to the judgment of each CPCU to decide, in the light of his or her occupational position, the content and form of continuing education that will satisfy the ethical obligation under *R2.1*.

G2.3 A number of other professions have established mandatory continuing education requirements, under the terms of which a member usually faces severe penalties unless he or she periodically certifies that at least one of the specified continuing education options has been met. At present and for the foreseeable future, the Trustees of the American Institute have no plans to require CPCUs to certify periodically that they have met the obligations under *Rule R2.1*. However, because the maintenance of professional competence is considered a minimum obligation of every CPCU, it has been given the status of a *Rule* under the *Code*. The Board of Ethical Inquiry will investigate alleged violations of *Rule R2.1*, and it may impose upon violators such penalties as are warranted. Furthermore, if a CPCU is accused of violating any other *Rule* in the *Code*, the Board may, at its discretion, require the accused to furnish evidence of compliance with *Rule R2.1*.

G2.4 Beyond the minimum continuing education requirements referred to in *Rule R2.1*, all CPCUs are urged to engage in such additional pursuits as will meet the aspirational goal, under *Canon 2*, of *improving* their professional knowledge, skills, and competence.

For example, the Board of Ethical Inquiry suggests that every CPCU should qualify for recognition under the Continuing Professional Development (CPD) program, which is jointly sponsored by the American Institute and the CPCU Society.

The CPD program recognizes those who have met specific criteria. The requirements of the CPD program, which are revised from time to time, are automatically distributed to CPCUs who are members of the CPCU Society and are available to others on request. Current criteria, with points assigned to various activities, include:

- Passing an exam or course in a nationally known insurance or business-related program.

- Passing a college or university course in insurance, risk management, or a business-related subject.

- Teaching a course in insurance, risk management, or a business-related subject.

- Authoring or co-authoring an article accepted for publication in the *CPCU Journal* or similar business publication, a CPCU Society section newsletter, or a textbook.

- Conducting a research project.

- Serving as an officer, director, committee chair, or committee member of a national insurance organization or local CPCU chapter.

- Serving as a class coordinator for a CPCU chapter or other course-sponsoring organization.

- Serving on a state insurance advisory committee.

- Grading IIA or CPCU exams.

- Serving on exam development committees for IIA, CPCU, state licensing, or other examination programs.

- Attending the CPCU Annual Meeting and Seminars or the annual meetings of other national insurance organizations.

- Attending educational meetings, seminars, videoconferences, or workshops sponsored by the CPCU Society or others.

- Attending meetings of CPCU chapters or other insurance organizations that include a speaker or an educational program.

- Meeting state continuing education requirements for licensing.

- Being an expert witness.

- Serving as a personal sponsor for CPCU and IIA students.

Continuous Learning for CPCUs

In 1997 the Board of Trustees of the American Institute reaffirmed its earlier position by adopting the following position.

1. We reaffirm that the Code of Professional Ethics of the American Institute requires all CPCUs to continue their professional development, as expressed in the *Statement on Continuous Learning* (below).

2. Because CPCUs are a diverse group with diverse learning needs, we reject the idea of a policing program to determine whether CPCUs have met a defined, measurable minimum standard.

3. We continue to support the Continuing Professional Development (CPD) program, jointly administered by the American Institute and the CPCU Society.

4. We intend to expand Institute services to help CPCUs maintain and enhance their knowledge in a rapidly changing, increasingly complex world.

Statement on Continuous Learning

Continuous learning has always been mandatory for CPCUs subject to the *Code*. *Rule R2.1* under *Canon 2* of the CPCU *Code of Professional Ethics* requires CPCUs to "keep informed on those technical matters that are essential to the maintenance of the CPCU's professional competence in insurance, risk management, or related fields." As pointed out in *Guideline G2.1*, "each and every CPCU has an ethical obligation to engage actively and continuously in appropriate educational activities."

Although the CPCU Society and the American Institute for CPCU jointly administer a voluntary Continuing Professional Development program, the American Institute has never imposed a mandatory reporting system for determining whether all CPCUs have complied with *Rule R2.1*. In fact, *Guideline G2.2* states that "it is left to the judgment of each CPCU to decide, in light of his or her occupational position, the content and form of continuing education that will satisfy the ethical obligation under *Rule R2.1*." However, *Guideline G2.3* allows the Board of Ethical Inquiry, while conducting investigations of other alleged violations of the *Code*, to "require the accused to furnish evidence of compliance with *Rule R2.1*."

Virtually any mandatory system that the American Institute could implement for determining whether CPCUs have complied with *Rule R2.1* would entail the use of an artificial minimum standard. Such a system, by emphasizing an artificial minimum, would serve to undermine the responsibility of each CPCU to identify and pursue "appropriate educational activities."

Canon 3

CPCUs should obey all laws and regulations, and should avoid any conduct or activity which would cause unjust harm to others.

Rules of Professional Conduct

R3.1   In the conduct of business or professional activities, a CPCU shall not engage in any act or omission of a dishonest, deceitful, or fraudulent nature.

R3.2   A CPCU shall not allow the pursuit of financial gain or other personal benefit to interfere with the exercise of sound professional judgment and skills.

R3.3   A CPCU shall not violate any law or regulation relating to professional activities or commit any felony.

Guidelines for Professional Conduct

G3.1   A CPCU should neither misrepresent nor conceal a fact or information which is material to determining the suitability, efficacy, scope, or limitations of an insurance contract or surety bond. Nor should a CPCU materially misrepresent or conceal the financial condition, or the quality of services, of any insurer or reinsurer. The extent to which a CPCU should volunteer information and facts must necessarily be left to sound professional judgment of what is required under the circumstances. This *Guideline* is intended to illustrate the kinds of acts and omissions which can be "dishonest, deceitful, or fraudulent," in violation of *Rule R3.1*, and which normally "would cause unjust harm to others," thus violating the spirit of *Canon 3*.

G3.2   A CPCU should not, to the detriment of the insuring public, engage in any business practice or activity designed to restrict fair competition. However, this *Guideline* does not prohibit a CPCU's participation in a legally enforceable covenant not to compete, in a rating bureau, or in a similar activity specifically sanctioned or required by law.

G3.3   In the performance of the CPCU's own occupational function, a CPCU should not deliberately achieve or seek to achieve, at the expense of the uninformed, financial gains for the CPCU, or the CPCU's employer, which are unconscionable relative to the customary gains for the quantity and quality of services actually rendered.

Generally, no CPCU should seek or accept compensation which is neither for nor commensurate with professional services actually rendered or to be rendered. Nor should any CPCU seek or accept compensation under any other terms, conditions, or circumstances which would violate any *Canon, Guideline,* or *Rule* in this *Code.* However, nothing in this *Guideline* is intended to prohibit the seeking or acceptance of gifts from family or personal friends, income from investments, or income from any other activity which would neither (a) prevent or inherently impair the free and complete exercise of the CPCU's sound professional judgment and skills nor (b) otherwise violate this *Code.*

A CPCU should not perform professional services under terms, conditions, or circumstances which would prevent or inherently impair the free and complete exercise of the CPCU's sound professional judgment and skills. This guideline does not prohibit a CPCU from being compensated under the terms of a legally acceptable commission arrangement since such an arrangement, in itself, does not prevent or inherently impair the CPCU's sound professional judgment and skills. But it does serve to remind a CPCU so compensated of his or her ethical obligation to avoid any recommendation to a consumer of the CPCU's services that would increase the CPCU's compensation, unless such recommendation clearly meets the consumer's legitimate needs and best interests. The guideline also serves to remind every CPCU, regardless of his or her basis of compensation, of the ethical obligation to render fully such services as are contemplated and rightfully owed under the terms of the applicable compensation arrangement.

G3.4   While the Institute's standards of ethical conduct are by no means limited to the duties and obligations imposed upon CPCUs by the laws and regulations which govern the conduct of all insurance practitioners, obedience to and respect for law and regulatory authority should be viewed as an absolute minimum standard of professional conduct below which no CPCU should fall. The potential consequences of violating this admonition extend beyond those which may fall upon the violator since one CPCU may indeed bring discredit upon the CPCU designation, and thus all who hold it, by violating laws or regulations which govern the conduct of a CPCU's business activities.

A CPCU is obligated to keep fully informed of each and every law and regulation governing or otherwise pertaining to his business activities.

In so doing, a CPCU should not hesitate to seek interpretive assistance from the appropriate regulatory officials and/or retain the services of competent legal counsel. When in doubt as to the legality of a particular kind of business conduct or activity, the CPCU should refrain from such conduct or activity.

A CPCU may not plead lack of knowledge as a defense for improper conduct under *Rule R3.3* unless the CPCU can demonstrate that he or she had made a reasonable effort in good faith to obtain such knowledge, and it was not available.

Canon 4

CPCUs should be diligent in the performance of their occupational duties and should continually strive to improve the functioning of the insurance mechanism.

Rules of Professional Conduct

R4.1   A CPCU shall competently and consistently discharge his or her occupational duties.

R4.2   A CPCU shall support efforts to effect such improvements in claims settlement, contract design, investment, marketing, pricing, reinsurance, safety engineering, underwriting, and other insurance operations as will both inure to the benefit of the public and improve the overall efficiency with which the insurance mechanism functions.

Guidelines for Professional Conduct

G4.1   From one who purports to be a true professional, the public has a right to expect both competence, in the sense of abilities, and diligent performance, in the sense of consistently applying those abilities in the service of others. Thus, to complement *Rule R2.1*, which obligates a CPCU to maintain professional competence by keeping informed, the Institute also promulgated *Rule R4.1*, which stipulates that "a CPCU shall competently and consistently *discharge* his or her occupational duties."

Although the Board of Ethical Inquiry earnestly believes that diligent performance should be an ethical obligation of all professionals, including CPCUs, the Board will not intervene or arbitrate between the parties in an employment or contractual relationship or civil dispute. Nor does the Board feel that the Institute's disciplinary procedures should become a substitute for legal and other remedies available to such parties. In the event of an alleged violation of *Rule R4.1*, therefore, the Board will hear the case only after all other remedies have been exhausted, and it generally will take disciplinary action only under circumstances where (1) a proven violation has caused unjust harm to another person, and the violation brings substantial discredit upon the CPCU designation; or (2) it would otherwise be in the *public* interest to take disciplinary action under the ethics code.

G4.2 In addition to competently and consistently discharging his or her own occupational duties, a CPCU is obligated by *Rule R4.2* to "support efforts to effect such improvements (in insurer functions and operations) as will both inure to the benefit of the public and improve the overall efficiency with which the insurance mechanism functions." Note that the obligation is to support the kinds of improvements which will *both* improve the efficiency of the insurance mechanism *and* benefit the public. The drafters of the *Code* worded the Rule in this fashion to focus attention on the fact that it is possible to effect improvements in insurer efficiency and profitability at least in the short run, in a manner contrary to the public interest. Granted, it is sometimes very difficult to determine whether a proposed change will both improve overall efficiency and inure to the benefit of the public, but the ethical obligation, consistent with the theme expressed in *Canon 1*, is to support *efforts* to effect such improvements. The kinds of efforts which satisfy both criteria, and which the Board feels a CPCU should support, are illustrated in the *Guidelines* immediately following.

G4.3 A CPCU should assist in improving the language, suitability, adaptability, and general efficacy of insurance contracts and surety bonds.

G4.4 A CPCU should assist in ensuring protection and security for the public, and in maintaining and improving the integrity of the insurance institution, by helping to preserve and improve the financial strength of all private insurers.

G4.5 A CPCU should assist in providing an adequate supply of insurance and surety bonds to meet public demands and needs.

G4.6 A CPCU should do the utmost to assist in minimizing the cost to the public of insurance and suretyship, without compromising the quality of benefits or services they provide, not only by helping to improve the operational efficiency of insurers and their representatives but also by contributing to the solution of economic, legal, political, and other social problems which demonstrably increase the cost of insurance and suretyship without enhancing their quality or otherwise improving the public well-being. Examples of such problems include, though are not limited to, inflation, unemployment, crime, inequities and inefficiencies in our legal system, inequities and inefficiencies in our health care delivery system, riots, floods and other highly destructive natural catastrophes, and the physical deterioration of property in the nation's cities. The ready availability of insurance alone will not solve such problems. And a CPCU should not neglect his or her personal duty, as a good citizen and a professional, to become actively involved in the search for underlying causes of, and long-run solutions to, such problems.

G4.7   Because of a CPCU's professional capabilities and firsthand knowledge of a tragic magnitude of human and dollar losses suffered annually, a CPCU should assume an especially active role in private and public loss prevention and reduction efforts. A CPCU should do the utmost to preserve each and every human life, maintain and improve the physical and mental health of all human beings, and prevent the damage, destruction, and abstraction of property.

G4.8   A CPCU should make an effort to participate in and support research which promises to assist in improving the functioning of the private insurance mechanism and/or in reducing losses of life, health, or property.

G4.9   The ethical obligation under this *Code* to strive for improvement in the functioning of the private insurance mechanism does not bar a CPCU from serving in the public sector. Nor does it bar a CPCU, as an *individual* citizen, from supporting a governmental role in providing economic security for the citizenry. But a CPCU should be mindful of the restriction imposed by *Rule R8.4,* and should avoid even the appearance of speaking on behalf of the Institute, especially on political matters.

Canon 5

CPCUs should assist in maintaining and raising professional standards in the insurance business.

Rules of Professional Conduct

R5.1   A CPCU shall support personnel policies and practices which will attract qualified individuals to the insurance business, provide them with ample and equal opportunities for advancement, and encourage them to aspire to the highest levels of professional competence and achievement.

R5.2   A CPCU shall encourage and assist qualified individuals who wish to pursue CPCU or other studies which will enhance their professional competence.

R5.3   A CPCU shall support the development, improvement, and enforcement of such laws, regulations, and codes as will foster competence and ethical conduct on the part of all insurance practitioners and inure to the benefit of the public.

R5.4   A CPCU shall not withhold information or assistance officially requested by appropriate regulatory authorities who are investigating or prosecuting any alleged violation of the laws or regulations governing the qualifications or conduct of insurance practitioners.

Guidelines for Professional Conduct

G5.1   A CPCU should assist in the raising of professional standards in the insurance business. At a minimum, every CPCU should conduct his or her own business activities in a manner which will, by the CPCU's precept and example, inspire other practitioners to do likewise.

G5.2   Both the insuring public and the insurance industry will benefit from continued growth in the number of insurance practitioners who achieve a high level of professional attainment. Thus, *Rule R5.2* stipulates that "A CPCU shall encourage and assist qualified individuals who wish to pursue CPCU or other studies which will enhance their professional competence."

A CPCU should share with all other insurance practitioners, as well as fellow CPCUs, the benefits of the CPCU's professional attainments. A CPCU's conduct should be guided by a spirit of altruistic concern for the public interest, and the public interest is best served when all insurance practitioners are well informed.

Moreover, any professional who has acquired a unified body of knowledge is invariably indebted to innumerable predecessors and contemporaries for having made available the benefits of their professional attainments, that is, for having shared freely with others their knowledge, accumulated experiences, skills, and insights into understanding. So also should a CPCU, as a professional who has subscribed to high ethical standards, share freely with contemporaries and, thus, future generations, the benefits of his or her own professional attainments, apart from any hope or expectation of immediate financial gain, because of the CPCU's ethical obligations to repay an indebtedness to forebears, contribute to the efficient advancement of human knowledge, and manifest an altruistic concern for the public interest.

A CPCU should support and participate in educational activities which will assist other practitioners in their professional development. Examples of such activities include seminars, lectures, research projects, teaching, preparation of educational materials for training programs, and preparation of professional articles for professional or lay publications. In writing or speaking publicly as a CPCU, however, the CPCU should maintain the dignity and high professional standards appropriate to the designation.

This *Guideline* does not obligate a CPCU to divulge trade secrets or other information which would put the CPCU at a competitive disadvantage. Instead, it serves as a reminder that just as the truly professional physician demonstrates a commitment to the advancement of medicine by sharing his or her knowledge and experiences with other physicians and aspiring physicians, so also should a CPCU play a role in the development of the field of insurance, in part by sharing knowledge with other practitioners as well as students.

Canon 6

CPCUs should strive to establish and maintain dignified and honorable relationships with those whom they serve, with fellow insurance practitioners, and with members of other professions.

Rules of Professional Conduct

R6.1   A CPCU shall keep informed on the legal limitations imposed upon the scope of his or her professional activities.

R6.2   A CPCU shall not disclose to another person any confidential information entrusted to, or obtained by, the CPCU in the course of the CPCU's business or professional activities, unless a disclosure of such information is required by law or is made to a person who necessarily must have the information in order to discharge legitimate occupational or professional duties.

R6.3   In rendering or proposing to render professional services for others, a CPCU shall not knowingly misrepresent or conceal any limitations on the CPCU's ability to provide the quantity or quality of professional services required by the circumstances.

Guidelines for Professional Conduct

G6.1   First and foremost by exhibiting high levels of professional competence and ethical conduct, a CPCU should constantly strive to *merit* the confidence and respect of those whom they serve, fellow practitioners, and members of other professions.

G6.2   A CPCU should strive to establish and maintain dignified and honorable relationships with competitors, as well as with other fellow practitioners.

G6.3   A CPCU should strive to establish and maintain dignified and honorable relationships with members of other professions, including but not limited to law, medicine, and accounting. The insurance industry relies heavily on the expertise and cooperation of such professionals in fulfilling its obligation to deliver insurance benefits promptly and otherwise render high quality insurance services to the public.

G6.4   Like other professionals, a CPCU should maintain the knowledge and skills necessary to exercise independent judgment in the performance of his or her professional services. However, a CPCU should always be mindful of his or her personal limitations. A CPCU should not hesitate to seek the counsel of other professionals, therefore, not only at the request of those whom the CPCU may serve but also on the CPCU's own initiative, particularly in doubtful or difficult situations or when the quality of professional service may otherwise be enhanced by such consultation.

G6.5   A CPCU is obligated to keep fully informed on any and all legal limitations imposed upon the scope of his or her professional activities. A CPCU should always exercise caution to avoid engaging in, or giving the appearance of engaging in, the unauthorized practice of law. However, nothing herein should be construed as prohibiting the practice of law by a CPCU who is otherwise qualified by virtue of his or her admission to the bar.

G6.6   Beyond the obligations under *Rule R6.2*, a CPCU should exercise caution and sound judgment in dealing with any confidential or privileged information.

Canon 7

CPCUs should assist in improving the public understanding of insurance and risk management.

Rules of Professional Conduct

R7.1   A CPCU shall support efforts to provide members of the public with objective information concerning their risk management and insurance needs and the products, services, and techniques which are available to meet their needs.

R7.2   A CPCU shall not misrepresent the benefits, costs, or limitations of any risk management technique or any product or service of an insurer.

Guidelines for Professional Conduct

G7.1   Fulfillment of all the public's insurance needs would appreciably enhance the economic and social well-being of society. But the public's insurance needs can be fully met only if every citizen recognizes his or her insurance needs and appreciates the importance of seeking competent and ethical assistance in analyzing and meeting these needs. The achievement of this result requires the combined efforts of all knowledgeable insurance professionals. Accordingly, every CPCU should assist in every practical manner to improve the public understanding of insurance and risk management even if the CPCU does not specialize in insurance education, marketing, claims settlement, safety engineering, advertising, or other professional activities which provide frequent opportunities to communicate directly to the public.

G7.2   A CPCU should keep abreast of legislation, changing conditions and/ or other developments which may affect the insuring public and should assist in keeping the public informed of such.

G7.3   In order to contribute to a better public understanding of insurance and risk management, it is essential for every CPCU to maintain and improve his or her own knowledge and communicative skills. However, no CPCU should hesitate to admit freely that he or she does not know the answer to a question. Nor should a CPCU attempt to answer such a question if it lies outside the realm of the CPCU's professional competence, authority, or proper function.

G7.4   A CPCU should neither engage in nor condone deceptive advertising or business practices which significantly mislead the public or otherwise contribute to the widespread misunderstanding or misuse of insurance. The minimum goal of all a CPCU's communications with the public should be to provide objective and factual information.

G7.5   It is highly desirable for the public to recognize its overall risk management needs and the limitations and advantages of insurance in meeting such needs. For instance, a CPCU should seize every opportunity to stress the importance of loss prevention and reduction in any well-conceived risk management program.

G7.6   *Rule R7.1* stipulates that "A CPCU shall support efforts to provide members of the public with objective information concerning their risk management and insurance needs, and the products, services, and techniques which are available to meet their needs." Both in the *Rules* and in the *Guidelines* above, the needs referred to are those which exist (at a point in time, understood) and the products, services, and techniques referred to are those which are available (at a point in time, understood). Neither the *Rules* nor the *Guidelines* require a CPCU to support lobbying efforts or proposed legislation, or the taking of positions on controversial issues. Nor do any of the *Code* standards prohibit a CPCU from engaging in such activities, in his or her own name and as an individual. However, a CPCU who elects to engage in such activities should take great care to avoid violating *Rule R8.4*.

Canon 8

CPCUs should honor the integrity of the CPCU designation and respect the limitations placed on its use.

Rules of Professional Conduct

R8.1   A CPCU shall use the CPCU designation and the CPCU key only in accordance with the relevant *Guidelines* promulgated by the American Institute.

R8.2   A CPCU shall not attribute to the mere possession of the designation depth or scope of knowledge, skills, and professional capabilities greater than those demonstrated by successful completion of the CPCU program.

R8.3   A CPCU shall not make unfair comparisons between a person who holds the CPCU designation and one who does not.

R8.4   A CPCU shall not write, speak, or act in such a way as to lead another to reasonably believe the CPCU is officially representing the American Institute, unless the CPCU has been duly authorized to do so by the American Institute.

Guidelines for Professional Conduct

G8.1   *Rule R8.1* of the *Code of Professional Ethics* stipulates that "A CPCU shall use the CPCU designation and the CPCU key only in accordance with the relevant *Guidelines* promulgated by the American Institute." These *Guidelines*, which define and impose restrictions upon the privilege to use the CPCU designation and key, are set forth below. They are designed to prevent undignified commercialization of the designation, unfair comparisons with able and well-established insurance practitioners who do not hold the designation, and other unethical practices which are inconsistent with the professional concepts which CPCU represents. Specifically, every CPCU has an ethical obligation to comply with the following minimum standards:

   a.   The designation Chartered Property Casualty Underwriter, the initials CPCU, and the CPCU key may be used only in a dignified and professional manner.

      1.   The designation or initials may be used after the holder's name on business cards, stationery, office advertising, signed articles, business and professional listings, and telephone list-

        ings, except where such use would conflict with the provisions of subparagraph a.3. below.

2. The CPCU key (actual size or reduced, but not enlarged) may be imprinted only on business cards and stationery used exclusively by CPCUs. Copies of the CPCU key suitable for reproduction are available from the American Institute.

3. The CPCU designation being personal in nature, the designation itself, the initials CPCU, and the CPCU key are not to be used as part of a firm, partnership, or corporate name, trademark, or logo, or affixed to any object, product, property, for any purpose whatsoever, except by the American Institute.

b. The designation Chartered Property Casualty Underwriter, the initials CPCU, and the CPCU key may be used to announce the conferment of the designation.

1. News releases prepared by the American Institute are mailed to all new CPCU designees. Only these approved releases, with the addition of personal biographical information, may be used by individual CPCU designees in preparing material for the business and community press.

2. The American Institute encourages employers of new designees to publish in company publications articles congratulating the new designees. The American Institute's official listing of new designees, published at the time of the conferment ceremony, should be used to verify the names of new designees. Copies of the CPCU key are available from the American Institute for reproduction in such articles.

3. The American Institute encourages the appearance of dignified advertisements congratulating new designees on earning the CPCU designation. Copies of the CPCU key are available from the American Institute for reproduction in such advertisements. These advertisements must be strictly congratulatory in nature, however, and should not include the business conducted by the firm, the lines of insurance carried by the firm, the firm's telephone number, or any copy soliciting business.

c. The designation Chartered Property Casualty Underwriter, the initials CPCU, and the CPCU key may be used by the CPCU Society in a manner which complies with the *Rules* and *Guidelines* of the American Institute's *Code of Professional Ethics* and which has first been authorized in writing by the Ethics Counsel of the American Institute.

d. The designation Chartered Property Casualty Underwriter, the initials CPCU, and the CPCU key may not be used in any manner which violates a *Rule* of the *Code of Professional Ethics. Rules R8.2, R8.3,* and *R8.4* deserve special mention in this context since they relate directly to, and impose restrictions upon, the privilege to use the CPCU designation.

e. The designation Chartered Property Casualty Underwriter, the initials CPCU, and the CPCU key may be used in any other manner which has received prior approval in writing from the Ethics Counsel of the American Institute.

Any questions regarding the interpretation of these *Guidelines* should be directed to the American Institute's Board of Ethical Inquiry. A prompt response will be made to all such requests.

G8.2 *Rule R8.2* stipulates that "A CPCU shall not attribute to the *mere possession of the designation* [emphasis supplied] depth or scope of knowledge, skills, and professional capabilities greater than those demonstrated by successful completion of the CPCU program." Unless this *Rule* is strictly observed by all CPCUs, the public will be misled and the integrity of the designation, as well as the integrity of the violator, will be significantly diminished.

CPCUs can be justifiably proud of having passed the rigorous qualifying exams and of having met the ethical and experience requirements imposed by the American Institute. But the CPCU curriculum, comprehensive though it is, does not in itself make a person an expert in every insurance and insurance-related area. Moreover, the CPCU curriculum has been periodically altered over the years to accommodate revised educational needs and objectives.

Consider, for instance, the case of an agent whose CPCU designation was conferred in a year prior to 1978. Such an agent would clearly violate *R8.2* if he or she led a prospective client to believe that the possession of the CPCU designation made him or her a qualified expert in life, health, or group insurance, particularly since the curriculum at that time provided little or no study or testing in these areas. The agent might otherwise have become a qualified expert in life, health, or group insurance, perhaps through experience and/or other formal educational programs, but it would be unethical to attribute this expertise to his or her possession of the CPCU designation per se. In short, the public is protected and the integrity of the designation and its holder are best preserved by avoiding any misrepresentations of the nature and significance of the CPCU designation.

Canon 9

CPCUs should assist in maintaining the integrity of the *Code of Professional Ethics*.

Rules of Professional Conduct

R9.1   A CPCU shall not initiate or support the CPCU candidacy of any individual known by the CPCU to engage in business practices which violate the ethical standards prescribed by this *Code*.

R9.2   A CPCU possessing unprivileged information concerning an alleged violation of this *Code* shall, upon request, reveal such information to the tribunal or other authority empowered by the American Institute to investigate or act upon the alleged violation.

R9.3   A CPCU shall report promptly to the American Institute any information concerning the use of the CPCU designation by an unauthorized person.

Guidelines for Professional Conduct

G9.1   It is *not* an objective of the American Institute to achieve growth in the number of CPCUs at the expense of professional standards, but rather to encourage more qualified individuals to meet the high standards which have always characterized the CPCU designation requirements. A CPCU should assist in upholding the experience, educational, and ethical standards prescribed for prospective CPCU designees by the American Institute for Chartered Property Casualty Underwriters.

G9.2   A CPCU should assist the American Institute in preserving the integrity of the *Code of Professional Ethics*, first and foremost by *voluntarily* complying with both the letter and the spirit of the *Code*. Ultimately, however, the public can be protected and the integrity of the *Code* can be maintained only if the *Code* is strictly but fairly enforced, and this, in turn, can be achieved only if *Code* violations are promptly brought to the attention of the proper officials. Although a CPCU should not become a self-appointed investigator or judge on matters properly left to the Board of Ethical Inquiry, every CPCU should comply with the mandates of *Rules R9.1, R9.2,* and *R9.3*. Except for the comparatively rare but troublesome situation covered by *R9.3*, whether a CPCU should *volunteer* adverse information is left to the judgment of the CPCU.

G9.3   Upon request, a CPCU should serve on such committees, boards, or tribunals as are prescribed by the Institute for the administration or enforcement of the *Code*. A CPCU is obligated to disqualify himself or herself from such service (i) if the CPCU believes, in good conscience, that he or she could not serve in a fair and impartial manner or (ii) upon request.

Disciplinary Rules, Procedures, and Penalties for the Enforcement of the Code of Professional Ethics of the American Institute for Chartered Property Casualty Underwriters

I. Applicability

A. In accordance with Articles I and IV of the Bylaws of the American Institute, the Board of Trustees has established educational, experience, and ethics standards which must be met by every individual who seeks the privilege of being designated a Chartered Property Casualty Underwriter (CPCU). The ethical standards are set forth explicitly in the *Code of Professional Ethics*.

The *Code* consists of two kinds of standards, *Canons* and *Rules of Professional Conduct*. Whereas the *Canons* are general standards of an aspirational and inspirational nature, the *Rules* are specific standards of a mandatory and enforceable nature. The *Rules* prescribe the absolute minimum level of ethical conduct required of every individual subject to the *Code*.

B. Pursuant to the agreements stipulated in the application for admission to CPCU candidacy, all CPCU candidates voluntarily agree to be judged by the ethics standards prescribed by the Board of Trustees. Thus, at the time they matriculate with the American Institute and thereafter for as long as they remain candidates, all CPCU candidates are subject to the binding effect of the Rules of Professional Conduct.

C. The *Rules of Professional Conduct* are also enforceable and binding upon all CPCUs whose designations are conferred after July 1976. However, by resolution of the Board of Trustees, the earliest enforcement date shall be deferred for such CPCUs until 1 July 1977.

D. As respects CPCUs whose designations were conferred prior to July 1976, the earliest enforcement date shall be deferred until the first day following the filing, if any, of an individual CPCU's voluntary written election to be bound by the *Rules of Professional Conduct* or, if later, 1 July 1977.

II. Jurisdiction

A. The investigation of an alleged violation of the *Code of Professional Ethics* shall be carried out by a person or persons designated by the Chairman of the Board of Ethical Inquiry.

B. As authorized by the Bylaws, adjudication of alleged violations of the *Rules of Professional Conduct* shall be by the Board of Ethical Inquiry and the Ethics Policy Committee.

III. Ethics Policy Committee, Board of Ethical Inquiry, Ethics Counsel

A. ***Ethics Policy Committee of the Board of Trustees.*** The Board of Trustees of the American Institute shall select from its members an Ethics Policy Committee. The President shall designate one of the elected members as Chairman of this committee. The Ethics Policy Committee shall have responsibility for reviewing matters of policy associated with all Institute ethics activities, making recommendations to the Executive Committee and the Board of Trustees, and providing for liaison with the CPCU Society on ethical policy considerations. The Ethics Policy Committee shall promulgate the specific disciplinary procedures and penalties to be used in enforcing the *Code of Professional Ethics* of the American Institute and shall have the authority to approve such periodic changes in the disciplinary procedures and penalties as may be necessary or desirable. The Ethics Policy Committee shall also have the authority to act on behalf of the Board of Trustees on all recommendations of the Board of Ethical Inquiry concerning disciplinary matters. All revocations and suspensions of the privilege to use the CPCU designation shall be reported in writing to the Board.

B. ***Board of Ethical Inquiry.*** The Board of Ethical Inquiry shall consist of eight (8) members appointed by the President of the American Institute subject to the advice and consent of the Ethics Policy Committee. All members shall be CPCUs, and together they shall constitute, as nearly as is practical, a representative cross section of the occupational backgrounds and other pertinent characteristics of all CPCUs. One member shall be the Ethics Counsel, a staff officer of the American Institute other than the President, who shall serve ex officio as nonvoting chairperson. The other seven (7) members shall not be full-time employees of the American Institute or the CPCU Society.

When the Board of Ethical Inquiry is first selected, two of its voting members shall be appointed for a term of one year, two for a term of two years, and three for a term of three years. All terms thereafter shall be for three years, and no voting member shall serve for more than two full consecutive terms. Except for the members comprising the first Board of Ethical Inquiry, the terms of new members shall commence on the first day of January, and four members shall constitute a quorum.

The Board of Ethical Inquiry shall be responsible for implementing established and approved ethics policy. The principal functions of the Board of Ethical Inquiry shall be to certify that CPCU candidates have met all ethics requirements, issue opinions to CPCUs and CPCU candidates who request assistance in interpreting or applying the *Code of Professional Ethics*, instigate independent investigations of the facts in cases involving alleged *Rule* violations under the *Code*, and serve as the tribunal to hear and decide cases involving alleged *Rule* violations.

The Board of Ethical Inquiry shall, when it deems appropriate, (1) promulgate and publish guidelines to supplement the *Code of Professional Ethics*; (2) summarize and publish the rulings of the tribunal in cases brought before it; (3) recommend amendments and additions to the *Code*, improvements in the disciplinary and enforcement procedures, changes in ethics policy; and (4) engage in such other activities which will assist in the implementation of approved ethics policies. The Board of Ethical Inquiry may carry out some of its functions through Institute staff, consultants, investigators, or subcommittees, but all disciplinary actions and published materials must be approved by a majority of its voting members.

The Chairperson of the Board of Ethical Inquiry shall be the Ethics Counsel of the American Institute, who shall be the administrative head of the Board and shall preside at all meetings of the Board, but the chairperson may not participate in the deliberations of the Board in its capacity as a disciplinary tribunal.

C. **Ethics Counsel.** Ethics Counsel, hereinafter referred to as Counsel, in addition to the duties described in III. B. above, shall have the power and duty to

(1) investigate all matters involving an alleged violation of the *Code*;

(2) dispose of all matters (subject to the provisions of IV. B. and C. below) either by dismissal or the prosecution of formal charges before a Hearing Panel or the Ethics Policy Committee of the Board of Trustees;

(3) appear at hearings conducted with respect to petitions for reinstatement by CPCUs whose designations have been suspended or revoked; cross-examine witnesses testifying in support of the motion and marshal available evidence, if any, in opposition thereto; and

(4) maintain permanent records of all ethics matters processed and the disposition thereof.

IV. Procedures

A. *Complaints.*

(1) All complaints alleging a violation of the *Code of Professional Ethics* shall be submitted in writing to Counsel and signed by the complainant.

(2) If, after the investigation described in paragraph B. below, it is decided to proceed with formal disciplinary proceedings, a copy of the complaint shall be furnished by Counsel to the person or persons against whom the complaint is lodged.

(3) Counsel, in accordance with procedures specified below, shall determine whether the complaint is of sufficient merit to warrant submission to the Board of Ethical Inquiry.

B. *Procedures Concerning Alleged Violation of the Code by CPCUs.*

(1) *Investigation.* All investigations, whether upon complaint or otherwise, shall be initiated and conducted by Counsel. Upon the conclusion of an investigation, Counsel may dismiss complaints which, in Counsel's opinion, are frivolous, prima facie without merit, or for the lack of jurisdiction. The dismissal of any other complaint by Counsel may be effected only after Counsel has secured the concurrence of two voting members of the Board of Ethical Inquiry. Counsel shall submit to the Hearing Panel of the Board of Ethical Inquiry all other complaints which are not dismissed for the reasons contained herein.

(2) *Formal Hearing.* Formal disciplinary proceedings before a Hearing Panel of the Board of Ethical Inquiry shall be commenced by setting forth the specific charges of misconduct. A copy of such charges shall be served on the respondent and/or the respondent's attorney. In the event the respondent fails to file an answer within thirty days after service of the charges, it shall be assumed that the respondent does not intend to contest the charge, and the Hearing Panel shall make its decision based solely on the evidence submitted by Counsel. If the respondent files an answer and requests the opportunity to be heard in person, Counsel, after consultation with the Hearing Panel, shall fix the date and place of a hearing, giving the respondent at least fifteen days' notice thereof. The notice of hearing shall advise the respondent that the respondent is entitled to be represented by counsel, and to present evidence in his own behalf. Unless the opportunity to appear personally is specifically requested by the respondent or Counsel, there shall be no formal hearing held, and the complaint, defense, and any evidence ("the record") shall be submitted by Counsel to the Hearing Panel by mail. The members of the Hearing Panel may consider the matter by means of personal conference, correspondence, telephone, or other means of communication.

The Hearing Panel shall consist of three voting members of the Board of Ethical Inquiry selected by Counsel, one of whom shall be selected by Counsel to serve as Chairperson. In selecting the members of such a Hearing Panel, Counsel shall be guided by (1) the geographical proximity of the residence of a member to the residence of the respondent and (2) the availability of such member for service. A member so selected shall disclose any fact or circumstance causing him or her to believe that, for a conflict of interests or other meritorious reason, he or she should be disqualified from serving on such Panel. Within thirty days after the conclusion of the hearing, the Hearing Panel shall submit its report to the entire Board of Ethical Inquiry. The report shall summarize the evidence and contain the recommendations of its majority and any minority opinion. The majority vote of all voting members of the Board of Ethical Inquiry voting shall determine the acceptance or rejection of the recommendation of the Hearing Panel.

In those disciplinary matters which must be reviewed by, or which are appealed to, the Ethics Policy Committee ("the Committee"), Counsel shall submit the record, including the decision of the Board of Ethical Inquiry to the Chairperson of the Committee by mail. The respondent will be conclusively deemed to have waived all objections to the findings and recommendations of the Board of Ethical Inquiry unless the respondent had filed an answer upon service of the initial charges and notice of the institution of formal disciplinary proceedings before a Hearing Panel of the Board of Ethical Inquiry, as provided above. There shall be no formal hearing, and the Committee may make its decision on the record by means of personal conference, correspondence, telephone, or other means of communication. The Committee shall either approve, disapprove, or modify the recommendation of the Board of Ethical Inquiry within thirty days after the submission of the record by Counsel.

(3) A CPCU convicted by verdict, guilty plea, or plea of nolo contendere of any crime that violates the Rules of Professional Conduct immediately loses the right to use the CPCU designation. Such suspension of the right to use the CPCU designation shall last indefinitely, or until the convicted party petitions the Board of Ethical Inquiry and convinces the Board of that party's fitness again to use the designation.

C. *Procedure for Disciplinary Proceedings Involving Applicants for the CPCU Program.* Whenever Counsel determines that an applicant for the CPCU Program may have violated the *Code of Professional Ethics*, Counsel shall recommend, after investigation and in accord with the procedures herein, whether or not such applicant shall be approved or rejected.

(1) In cases where the alleged Code violation involves the breach of *Rule R3.3* of the *Code* or the suspension of a business or professional license, but where it appears that the applicant has been fully rehabilitated, Counsel shall secure the concurrence of two members of the Board of Ethical Inquiry before Counsel may authorize the acceptance of such application. If either of such members disagrees with Counsel's recommendation, the matter shall be submitted to a Hearing Panel in the same manner as a disciplinary matter referred to in IV. B. above.

(2) If the disciplinary matter involves an alleged *Code* violation other than the types described in IV. C. (1) above, and where Counsel, after investigation, determines that the applicant has been fully rehabilitated, counsel shall secure the concurrence of two CPCU members of the Executive Council of the American Institute for Chartered Property Casualty Underwriters before Counsel may authorize the acceptance of such application. If either of such members disagrees with

Counsel's recommendation, the matter shall be submitted to a Hearing Panel in the same manner as a disciplinary matter referred to in IV. B. above.

(3) If, after investigation, Counsel determines that the application should be rejected, Counsel shall advise the applicant in writing that the application will be submitted to a Hearing Panel of the Board of Ethical Inquiry with the recommendation that it be rejected. If the applicant contests the proposed recommendation, the applicant shall notify Counsel in writing, within thirty days of the receipt of such notice, of the desire to contest the recommendation together with any defense or evidence on the applicant's behalf. Counsel shall then submit the matter to a Hearing Panel in the same manner as a disciplinary matter referred to in IV. B. above. Unless the opportunity to appear personally is specifically requested by the respondent or Counsel, there shall be no formal hearing held, and the complaint, defense, and any evidence ("the record") shall be submitted by Counsel to the Hearing Panel by mail. The members of the Hearing Panel may consider the matter by means of personal conference, correspondence, telephone, or other means of communication. Within thirty days after the conclusion of the hearing, the Hearing Panel shall submit its report to the entire Board of Ethical Inquiry. The report shall summarize the evidence and contain the recommendation of its majority and any minority opinion.

(4) If the decision of the majority of the Board of Ethical Inquiry is to reject the application, the applicant shall have thirty (30) days within which to request a review of the decision by the Ethics Policy Committee, such review to be considered in the same manner as disciplinary matters referred to in IV. B. (2) above.

D. *Procedure for Disciplinary Proceedings Involving Candidates for the CPCU Program.* Whenever Counsel determines that a candidate for the CPCU Program may have violated the *Code of Professional Ethics*, Counsel shall recommend, after investigation and in accord with the procedures herein, whether or not such candidate shall be approved or disapproved.

(1) In cases where the alleged *Code* violation involves the breach of *Rule R3.3* of the *Code* or the suspension of a business or professional license, but where it appears that the candidate has been fully rehabilitated, Counsel shall secure the concurrence of two members of the Board of Ethical Inquiry in the continuation of the candidacy in good standing of such candidate. If either of such members disagrees with

Counsel's recommendation, the matter shall be submitted to a Hearing Panel in the same manner as a disciplinary matter referred to in IV. B. above.

(2) If the disciplinary matter involves an alleged *Code* violation other than the types described in IV. D. (1) above, and where Counsel, after investigation, determines that the candidate has been fully rehabilitated, Counsel shall secure the concurrence of two members of the Management Council of the American Institute for Chartered Property Casualty Underwriters in continuation of the candidacy in good standing of such candidate. If either of such members disagrees with Counsel's recommendation, the matter will be submitted to a Hearing Panel in the same manner as a disciplinary matter referred to in IV. B. above.

(3) If, after investigation, Counsel determines that the candidacy in good standing of such candidate should be terminated, Counsel shall advise the candidate in writing that the matter will be submitted to a Hearing Panel of the Board of Ethical Inquiry with the recommendation to terminate the candidacy.

If the candidate contests the proposed recommendation, the candidate shall notify Counsel in writing, within thirty days of the receipt of such notice, of the desire to contest the recommendation together with any defense or evidence on the candidate's behalf. Counsel shall then submit the matter to a Hearing Panel in the same manner as a disciplinary matter referred to in IV. B. above. Unless the opportunity to appear personally is specifically requested by the respondent or Counsel, there shall be no formal hearing held, and the complaint, defense, and any evidence ("the record") shall be submitted by Counsel to the Hearing Panel by mail. The members of the Hearing Panel may consider the matter by means of personal conference, correspondence, telephone, or other means of communication. Within thirty days after the conclusion of the hearing, the Hearing Panel shall submit its report to the entire Board of Ethical Inquiry. The report shall summarize the evidence and contain the recommendation of its majority and any minority opinion.

(4) If the majority of the Board of Ethical Inquiry rejects the application, the candidate shall have thirty (30) days within which to request a review of the decision by the Ethics Policy Committee. Such review would be considered in the same manner as disciplinary matters referred to in IV. B. (2) above.

(5) A candidate convicted by verdict, guilty plea, or plea of nolo contendere of any crime that violates the Rules of Professional Conduct is immediately suspended from further participation in the CPCU program. Such suspension shall last indefinitely, or until the convicted party petitions the Board of Ethical Inquiry and convinces the Board of that party's fitness again to participate in the CPCU program.

V. Penalties

A. If the Board of Ethical Inquiry determines that a complaint merits disciplinary action, it may impose or recommend, as appropriate, any penalty hereinafter described, *provided* that the severity of the penalty imposed shall be commensurate with the severity of the offense committed. The Board of Ethical Inquiry may also consider all the circumstances surrounding the commission of any offense and the likelihood that the offender has been rehabilitated. All penalties recommended by the Board of Ethical Inquiry must be reviewed, before becoming effective, by the Ethics Policy Committee and approved or modified as appropriate.

B. Penalties which may be administered in appropriate cases are as follows:

(1) with respect to CPCUs subject to the *Code:*

    (a) private admonitions, requesting the violator to cease and desist;

    (b) reprimands in the form of informal rebukes given limited publication;

    (c) censures in the form of formal rebukes given wide publication; and

    (d) revocation or suspension of the privilege to use the CPCU designation, for a probationary period or indefinitely, with or without publication.

(2) with respect to CPCU applicants and candidates, admission to any examination may be denied, and awarding of the CPCU designation may be withheld pending receipt of convincing proof of the candidate's full and complete rehabilitation.

C. All proceedings involving allegations of breach of the *Rules of Professional Conduct* shall be kept confidential except as to the parties, but penalties assessed and decisions made may be disclosed, provided the publication of disciplinary sanctions to others shall be approved by the Ethics Policy Committee.

VI. Miscellaneous Provisions

A. (1) Complaints against members of the Board of Ethical Inquiry or Counsel involving alleged violation of the *Rules of Professional Conduct* by them shall be submitted directly to the Ethics Policy Committee.

   (2) Complaints against members of the Ethics Policy Committee involving alleged violations of the *Rules of Professional Conduct* by them shall be submitted directly to the Board of Trustees of the American Institute for Chartered Property Casualty Underwriters.

B. Amendments to these Disciplinary Rules, Procedures, and Penalties shall bear their effective date as determined by the Ethics Policy Committee.

Effective 31 August 1976, as amended 17 June 1983,
12 June 1984, 16 February 1990, 16 June 1995, and
14 April 1999

Edwin S. Overman, Ph.D., CPCU
Chairman
Ethics Policy Committee

Hypothetical Case Studies of the Board of Ethical Inquiry

One of the most important functions of the Board of Ethical Inquiry is to facilitate voluntary compliance with the standards which are set forth in the *Code of Professional Ethics*. Accordingly, the Board periodically publishes *Guidelines* and *Advisory Opinions*. Whenever questions of interpretation arise, CPCUs and CPCU candidates are strongly encouraged to request *Advisory Opinions*. Only the Board of Ethical Inquiry is authorized to issue such opinions on behalf of the American Institute.

Unpublished opinions are informal and intended solely for the guidance of the individuals to whom they are issued, whereas published *Opinions* are formal and intended for the guidance of all persons subject to the *Code*. Each published *Opinion*, except those identified with the prefix "HCS," below, has a specified effective date after which it may be used in interpreting and applying the *Rules of Professional Conduct*. Such effective date for *Opinions HCS-101* through *HCS-122* is 1 June 1978.

Published *Opinions* are presented in the form of the Board's responses to hypothetical case studies. The cases and the corresponding *Opinions*, which are designated by the initials "HCS" and numbered for ease of reference, are "hypothetical" in the sense that they did not arise from actual disciplinary proceedings. Instead, inquiries of general import are edited, combined, and otherwise fabricated into imaginary case situations in which persons and organizations are referred to by fictitious names. The hypothetical nature of the cases preserves the anonymity of inquirers and provides an efficient means of posing a wide variety of ethical questions and issues to which the *Code* may be applied. The Board's *Opinions* anticipate and resolve such questions and issues in advance, thereby helping to prevent conduct which would be unethical and contrary to the public interest.

The Board's published *Opinions* are necessarily based on abbreviated case summaries and assumptions that are designed to maximize their educational value. It should therefore be obvious that published *Opinions* might differ appreciably from the decisions rendered in actual disciplinary proceedings since the latter decisions would be based on thorough investigations and hearings of the actual facts, evidence, and circumstances involved. Nonetheless, as official interpretations and applications of the *Rules of Professional Conduct*, the *Opinions* offer useful guidance for CPCUs and CPCU candidates.

CASE HCS-101

Mr. Richard Roe, in completing his matriculation application for the CPCU program, provided complete information regarding his past record of criminal convictions. Further investigation confirmed that Mr. Roe had received his high school diploma in 1972 while confined to a juvenile correctional institution for several counts of shoplifting, disorderly conduct, assaulting his foster parents, and resisting arrest. Within six weeks after his probationary release from the juvenile institution, Mr. Roe was arrested and charged with soliciting for a prostitute and armed robbery. He was convicted on both counts and served ten years in prison. In 1982, after careful consultation with the warden of the state penitentiary, the personnel director of an insurance company hired Mr. Roe to work in the company's printing shop. Seven years later, Mr. Roe, having successfully completed the IIA Program in General Insurance, was promoted to the position of underwriting trainee. He has since advanced to the position of junior underwriter to the "special risks" department and has been promised another promotion if he is able to fulfill the CPCU designation requirements. The personnel director, a CPCU, indicated that he would support Mr. Roe's candidacy. Mr. Roe is now married, is forty-seven years of age, and has two children. He is the coach of a little league baseball team and spends two Saturdays each month doing volunteer work at the local home for underprivileged children of deceased parents. Should Mr. Roe's application for the CPCU program be approved? Did the personnel director violate the ethics *Code?* Suppose Mr. Roe had not revealed his criminal record at the time he applied to the Institute, but the Institute discovered the true facts after Roe passed all the exams and met the experience requirements and before the national conferment ceremonies. Should Roe's CPCU designation be conferred?

OPINION HCS-101

Though alleged ethics violations are best interpreted in the context of the entire *Code of Professional Ethics* and related published materials, the standards most directly applicable to the Richard Roe Case are the *Preamble, Rules R3.3* and *R9.1,* and *Guideline G3.4.*

As clearly specified in the *Preamble* to the *Code,* and in the agreements an individual must sign at the time of applying for matriculation into the CPCU program, "all CPCU *candidates* [emphasis supplied] become subject to the binding effect of the *Rules* at the time they matriculate with the American Institute, and thereafter for as long as they remain candidates."

The facts reveal that Mr. Roe had violated the spirit of *Canon 3* and G3.4 on a number of occasions in the past, both by violating laws and by engaging in activity which caused unjust harm to others. But since no disciplinary action can be taken against any person not subject to the *Code*, and in the absence of a *Rule* violation, the issue here is whether Mr. Roe violated *R3.3*. Based on the nature and number of crimes committed, the Board feels that the answer must be yes. Mr. Roe did violate *R3.3* and is subject to disciplinary action.

Despite the foregoing, the Board would vote to admit Mr. Roe to CPCU candidacy. The published *Disciplinary Rules and Procedures* provide that such action may be taken "where it appears that the candidate has been fully rehabilitated." The evidence presented in the hypothetical case, though limited, persuades us to believe that Mr. Roe has been fully rehabilitated, and that he should not be made to suffer the rest of his life for crimes he committed long ago, and for which he has already been punished, as long as he continues to comply strictly with the *Code*.

Had Mr. Roe misrepresented the facts about his criminal record, and had the Institute discovered the misrepresentation before the designation was conferred, the Board would withhold the designation since the misrepresentation would be a violation of *R3.1* and would also be rather strong evidence that he was not fully rehabilitated. Mr. Roe would then be given an opportunity at some later date to offer convincing proof of full rehabilitation. Had Mr. Roe already received the designation, the Board of Ethical Inquiry would recommend to the Ethics Policy Committee that Mr. Roe's privilege to use the designation be suspended.

In the opinion of the Board, the personnel director did not violate *R9.1*. He did initiate and support Mr. Roe's CPCU candidacy, but he had no reason to suspect Roe "to engage in" (at the present time) business practices which violate the *Code*. The personnel director observed the spirit of *G9.2* when he avoided becoming a "self-appointed investigator or judge on matters properly left to the Board" and, we assume, by advising Roe to disclose his criminal record. Moreover, the personnel director seemed to be complying fully with *R5.1* while helping to deal with a serious social challenge, jobs for deserving ex-convicts, which the Board thinks is in the spirit of *Canon 1*.

CASE HCS-102

Mr. J. B. White, CPCU, LL.B., is regional claims manager for a large liability insurer. After reviewing a particular property damage liability claim, Mr. White agrees with Alan Adjuster that Mrs. Claimant is justifiably entitled to a settlement of $2,000. However, White instructs Adjuster to offer her $1,200 and a box of good chocolates. "If Mrs. Claimant refuses," White said, "explain to her that if she hires an attorney, his fee will be up to 50 percent of the settlement amount so if she takes our offer she will be $200 ahead of the game. If she still refuses, put the file in your desk drawer for a couple of months. She will eventually see it our way because she really needs the money." Mrs. Claimant later writes to the Board of Ethical Inquiry and argues that White and Adjuster are guilty of ethics violations. Adjuster says he was just following the orders of his superior. White says his action was "in accord with customary industry practices and, anyway, he "did not understand the *Rule of Conduct*, though he had glanced at the Institute's *Code of Professional Ethics* several times." Adjuster is not yet a CPCU, but he has matriculated and passed two of the CPCU examinations.

OPINION HCS-102

It bears repeating that alleged ethics violations are best interpreted in the context of the entire *Code of Professional Ethics* and of all the *Guidelines, Advisory Opinions,* and *Summaries of Previous Rulings* which have been approved by the Board of Ethical Inquiry and published by the American Institute. However, the standards most directly applicable to the J. B. White-Alan Adjuster Case are those contained in the *Preamble, Rules R1.1, R1.2, R2.1, R3.1, R3.3, R6.1, Guidelines G1.1, G1.2, G1.3, G1.4, G3.4,* and *Canons 1, 3,* and 6.

Here, as elsewhere, the Board of Ethical Inquiry is empowered to take or recommend disciplinary action only if the accused is (1) subject to the binding effect of the Rules and (2) guilty of a *Rule* violation.

Like all other CPCU candidates, Alan Adjuster is clearly bound by the *Rules* of the *Code*. Since he has already passed two of the national CPCU examinations, presumably he is a CPCU "candidate," that is, the American Institute had approved his matriculation application and granted him permission to take the examinations. The Institute would not have approved his matriculation application unless he had first signed an agreement to be bound by the ethics and other standards prescribed by the Institute. The applicability of the *Rules* to CPCU candidates is also stipulated in the *Preamble*.

Whether J. B. White is bound by the *Rules* depends on when his CPCU designation was conferred. He is bound by them automatically if his designation was conferred after July 1976, the effective date of the *Code*. But if his designation was conferred *before* July 1976, he is subject to the possibility of disciplinary action only if he voluntarily elects in writing to be bound unconditionally by the mandates of the Rules. For the purposes of this case, we will assume that Mr. White is subject to disciplinary action.

It is the opinion of the Board that both J. B. White and Alan Adjuster have violated several *Rules* of professional conduct. In jurisdictions which have so-called "Unfair Claims Practices Acts," the liability claims settlement approach of White and Adjuster may be contrary to statute and/or regulation, in which case it would likewise violate *R3.3* of the *Code*. Neither White nor Adjuster would be allowed to plead ignorance of such laws, for the reasons explained in *Guideline G3.4*, since the knowledge of such laws is readily available. Moreover, *Rule R6.1* very explicitly obligates them to "keep informed on the legal limitations imposed upon the scope of [their] professional activities." If the evidence confirmed that White and Adjuster were not aware of an applicable law governing the conduct of claims representatives, that alone would strongly suggest that they are also in violation of the minimum continuing education obligation, which is stipulated in *R2.1* and further clarified in *Guidelines G2.1* through *G2.4*.

Whether or not a statute or regulation had been violated, the Board believes that White and Adjuster did violate *R3.1*. The claims settlement approach in question may or may not meet all the narrow legal tests for "fraud" per se, but in a larger sense the approach is an act of a "dishonest and deceitful" *nature* within the intended meaning of the *Code* provisions since it is tantamount to cheating Mrs. Claimant out of the prompt, equitable, and otherwise fair treatment to which she is ethically entitled. Tactics of delay, bribery, and deliberate underpayment are contrary to the letter of *G1.4*. They clearly caused "unjust harm to others" within the meaning of *Canon 3*. They are flagrantly contrary to the *Canon 6* concept of establishing and maintaining "dignified and honorable relationships with those whom CPCUs serve," and they are clearly contrary to the "public interest" concept which constitutes the most fundamental goal of the entire *Code*, and which is set forth in *Canon 1* and *G1.1* through *G1.4*. While the *Canons and Guidelines* are not themselves enforceable, they can and will be used by the Board in interpreting the *Rules* and applying them to specific factual situations. Here, for instance, they clarify the intended meaning of *R3.1* and support the Board's conclusion that it was violated.

J. B. White's conduct is not excused by either alleged or actual ignorance of the *Code* because *R1.1* clearly gives him "a duty to understand and abide by all the *Rules*" and this is so regardless of whether such *Rules* are violated in practice by others who are not subject to the *Code*. Nor can White's conduct be excused by virtue of his having delegated the actual handling of the claim to Adjuster. White obviously violated *R1.2* by advocating, sanctioning, participating in, causing to be accomplished, carrying out through another or condoning an act which White is prohibited from performing under the *Rules*. Alan Adjuster's conduct is likewise in violation of *Rules R3.1, R3.3,* and *R6.1,* and *R1.2* makes it clear that such violations are not excused merely because the violator allegedly or actually followed the instructions of his superiors.

Although the members of the Board of Ethical Inquiry agree that both White and Adjuster engaged in conduct which is clearly unethical under the *Code*, additional evidence would be considered before determining the exact nature of the disciplinary actions to be taken. At a minimum, the Board would issue private admonitions to White and Adjuster. That is to say, a letter would be sent to each violator. It would notify each that the Board had ruled the conduct to be unethical. It would request each violator to cease and desist from engaging in such conduct, and it would forewarn each of the potential consequences of continuing *Rule* violations. If a violator failed to cease and desist, if he was later found guilty of additional violations, or if the original investigation and hearing process disclosed adverse evidence which is not apparent from the limited information given, the Board would probably impose or recommend stronger sanctions. Adjuster, a candidate, could have his CPCU designation withheld, for a probationary period or indefinitely, until such time that he provided convincing proof of his full and complete rehabilitation. J. B. White could be subject to reprimand, censure, or revocation or suspension of the privilege to use the CPCU designation (the latter would have to be approved by the Ethics Policy Committee of the Board of Trustees of the American Institute).

Mrs. Claimant, as a party directly involved, would be notified of the decision and the penalties imposed. She would also be told that the Board has no power to intervene on her behalf in any legal dispute with the insurer. The Board of Ethical Inquiry does have the power, at its discretion, to disclose the decisions and penalties to officers and Chapters of the CPCU Society, as well as to the parties directly involved. But any publication of sanctions to others, as in a public censure, must first be approved by the Ethics Policy Committee of the Board of Trustees.

CASE HCS-103

Jay Agent, CPCU, and Roger Partner, CPCU, are the owners and operators of a combination real estate and general insurance agency. In recent years Agent has been managing most of the insurance activities, while Partner has concentrated on the real estate portion of the business. Partner bought 500 acres of nearly worthless swampland for $5 an acre, instructed his secretary to run full-page ads in various senior citizen publications, eventually sold the land at an average of $4,000 for each half-acre plot, and split the total proceeds with Agent in accordance with the partnership agreement. A retired couple who had purchased one of the plots provided the Institute's Ethics Counsel with evidence that they bought the land only because the advertisement said the subdivision already had paved streets and sidewalks, city water, two swimming pools, tennis courts, a clubhouse, and free lifetime health care for the first twenty couples to buy at least one plot. None of these improvements and benefits were available when they arrived at the swamp with their mobile home. Agent contends that he personally did not violate the Code since the insurance aspects of the business were conducted legally and ethically. Partner contends that his real estate activities have nothing to do with insurance, and hence, his status as a CPCU.

OPINION HCS-103

The standards most directly applicable to the Jay Agent-Roger Partner Case are those contained in *Rules R1.1, R1.2, R3.1, R3.2, R3.3,* and *R6.1, Guidelines G1.2, G1.3, G3.3, G3.4,* and *Canons 1, 3,* and *6.* Though not specifically mentioned in the information given, it will be assumed that both Agent and Partner were bound by the *Rules*, either by voluntary election or by virtue of their CPCU conferment dates.

The Board is satisfied that the conduct of Jay Agent and Roger Partner was unethical. First, the evidence would undoubtedly confirm that one or more laws were violated (a breach of *R3.3*), and that the partners should have kept informed on such laws (in accord with *R6.1* and *G3.4*). Furthermore, it is clear that Partner's real estate scheme constituted "an act or omission of a dishonest, deceitful, or fraudulent nature" (thus violating the letter of *R3.1* and the spirit of *Canons 1, 3,* and 6), that the scheme raises serious questions about possible violations of *R3.2* (as clarified in *G3.3*), and that Agent and Partner have a duty to "*understand* and *abide* by *all* the *Rules*" as specified in *R1.1* [emphasis supplied]. Since there can be little doubt about the foregoing, the real issues here are as follows: Is Partner's real estate scheme outside the purview of the *Code*, as he contends? Does Agent's lack of direct involvement excuse his conduct? What disciplinary actions, if any, should be taken?

Roger Partner's real estate scheme is definitely within the purview of the *Code* and the jurisdiction of the Board. He is a CPCU. He is bound by the *Rules*. And *R3.1* clearly prohibits him from engaging in acts or omissions of a dishonest, deceitful, or fraudulent nature "in the conduct of business or professional activities." It does not say "insurance" activities. It says "business or professional activities," as intended by the drafters of the *Code*, and the phrase most certainly includes real estate activities. Roger Partner is also subject to disciplinary action, under *R3.3*, for the violation of "*any* law or regulation." Since the Board is disturbed by the serious nature of the offenses, the consequences to those harmed, and the likelihood of professional misconduct in the future, the Board would recommend that Roger Partner's privilege to use the CPCU designation be suspended indefinitely or revoked. The final decision would be made by the Ethics Policy Committee of the Board of Trustees.

Jay Agent's lack of direct involvement in the real estate scheme does not excuse the fact that he, too, was guilty of Rule violations. As stipulated in *R1.2*, "a CPCU shall not advocate, sanction, participate in, cause to be accomplished, otherwise carry out through another, or condone any act which the CPCU is prohibited from performing by the *Rules* of this *Code*. Even if Agent could prove that he did not advocate or participate in the illegal and fraudulent scheme, there is at least a rebuttable presumption that he condoned it by failing to object to the scheme and by accepting his share of the large sum of money involved. Surely a reasonable man would inquire into the source of a $2 million gain. But if Agent did not make such an inquiry, he would probably be guilty of complicity under the law, and he would also surely be in violation of *R3.2* (allowing the pursuit of financial gain to interfere with the exercise of sound professional judgment) and *R4.1* (failing to discharge his occupational duties competently). Accordingly, the Board would recommend to the Ethics Policy Committee that Agent's privilege to use the CPCU designation be suspended indefinitely or revoked.

If the Ethics Policy Committee agreed with the aforementioned recommendations, the decisions would undoubtedly be published widely, as well as conveyed to the complainants. If the final decision was to suspend the privilege to use the designation, both Agent and Partner would be given an opportunity at a later date to offer convincing proof of full and complete rehabilitation.

CASE HCS-104

Bob Broker, CPCU, is the brother of a powerful county politician who arranged for Bob to be broker-of-record on all insurance policies purchased by the county. Though the gross commission Bob receives on this insurance amounts to about $50,000 per year, virtually all of the everyday service work is performed by county and insurance company employees. Bob Broker's role is to place the coverage with the insurers on any cancellation or renewal dates, the coverage having been secured initially by a previous agent. Shortly before the renewal date of one of the policies, Broker obtained premium quotations from two insurers, A and B. Company B quoted a lower price and offered better coverages than Company A, but Broker selected Company A because it paid him a substantially higher commission rate (on a larger total premium). Although never explicitly requested to do so, Bob Broker contributed generously to his brother's political party, frequently entertained county employees on his yacht, and gave his brother the down payment for a new home. Bob's principal competitor, also a CPCU and a broker, reported all this information in a telephone conversation with the Institute's Ethics Counsel, but the competitor indicated that he did not want his name revealed, nor would he testify, in any disciplinary proceedings. He also said that "one of the county's insurers selected by Bob was rumored to be in financial trouble." Any code violations? Suppose a taxpayer brought the charges of ethical impropriety to the Institute.

OPINION HCS-104

In the case of Bob Broker, the first issue to be considered is the refusal of Competitor to testify or have his name used. Since one of the constitutional requirements of "due process" is the right of an accused to be confronted by his accuser(s), the American Institute's *Disciplinary Rules and Procedures* (sections IV. A., B.) provide that "all complaints alleging a violation of the *Code of Professional Ethics shall be submitted in writing to Counsel and signed by the complainant*" [emphasis supplied]. If Competitor refused to submit a complaint in writing and sign it, and if no other party was willing to do so, the complaint would be dismissed as frivolous and prima facie without merit. Any person may file a complaint against a CPCU or a CPCU candidate, as long as the complaint complies with the *Disciplinary Rules and Procedures*. However, if Bob Broker received his CPCU designation prior to July 1976 and he had not filed a voluntary written election to be bound by the *Rules*, the case would have to be dismissed for lack of jurisdiction.

Does Competitor's refusal to sign a complaint and testify constitute sufficient grounds for an ethics disciplinary action against him? While the Board notes with regret that Competitor's attitude is contrary to the aspirational goal of

Canon 9, there is no basis for a disciplinary action against him because he did not violate a *Rule* per se. *R9.2* does not obligate Competitor to sign a complaint or testify. It only obligates him to reveal, *upon request*, any information he may have concerning an alleged violation of the *Code*. Nor is he obligated to volunteer any information, except in the situation covered by *R9.3* (and clarified in *G9.2*). All CPCUs are encouraged to assist in maintaining the integrity of the *Code*; the reporting of adverse information is enough to prompt an investigation of the matter; the extent of a CPCU's involvement in any disciplinary proceedings is left largely to his or her own judgment; and the accused is protected from harassment and the deprivation of his rights. Achieving these objectives is a delicate task, perhaps even more so when, as in this case, the complainant is a competitor of the accused.

Assuming that the initial investigation eventually resulted in a proper complaint and sufficient evidence of possible misconduct to justify a formal hearing, the standards most directly applicable to Bob Broker would be *Rules R2.1, R3.1, R3.2, R3.3, R6.1, Guidelines G1.2, G3.1, G3.3,* and *G3.4,* and *Canons 1* and *3*.

It is entirely possible that the political contributions, entertainment, and/or down payment on his brother's home would meet the applicable tests for "rebating" commissions illegally, in which case Broker violated *R3.3* and would be subject to discipline. Though the Board obviously will not act solely on the basis of a rumor, if the evidence showed that Broker had recommended an insurer he knew to be in financial trouble, he clearly violated *R3.1* (a "dishonest, deceitful, or fraudulent" act, as clarified in *G3.1*).

If he did not know of the insurer's financial difficulties, it might open the avenue of inquiry into whether Bob Broker had complied with his minimum continuing education obligation under *R2.1*.

Broker's acceptance of commissions for work performed largely by others, though legal on its face, also raises the question of whether he violated the letter of *R3.2* or the spirit of *G1.2* and *G3.3*. The Board acknowledges that the acceptance of such compensation, which is not for and commensurate with services actually rendered or to be rendered, is contrary to the goals of *G1.2* and *G3.3*, but finds no evidence that such acceptance violated *R3.2*. However, the Board feels that Bob Broker probably did violate *R3.2*, as well as *R3.1*, by placing some of the insurance with the insurer who offered higher commissions and lesser coverages. This conclusion is amply supported by *G3.3*, though it obviously assumes that placing the insurance with the other insurer would have better met the consumer's legitimate needs and best interests, the actual determination of which would require additional information.

What disciplinary action, if any, should be taken against Bob Broker? While the investigation and hearings process might well prove to the contrary, it is apparent from the case that Broker may have violated as many as six *Rules* of professional conduct. If he were found guilty on all counts, the Board would recommend suspension of his privilege to use the CPCU designation. If he is found guilty on at least one but not all the counts, a lesser penalty might be imposed, especially if he had not violated any law.

CASE HCS-105

Joe President, CPCU, chief executive officer of a capital stock insurer, made a decision to cancel the agency contracts of all the company's agents in a particular state because of the poor loss ratio on auto insurance business. As a result, thousands of motorists had difficulty securing replacement coverage, and many ended up in the state's assigned risk plan. "My first and most important responsibility is to our stockholders," the president said when asked about the ethical propriety of his decision. "The rates in that state are not adequate to make a profit."

OPINION HCS-105

The standards most directly applicable to the Joe President Case are those contained in *Rules R1.1, R3.1, R3.3, R4.1, R4.2, Guidelines G1.1, G1.2, G1.3, G4.2,* and *Canons 1, 3, 4,* and *6.*

For the purpose of enhancing the educational value of this hypothetical case, the Board has assumed that a proper complaint has been filed, that Joe President is bound by the *Rules,* and that the complaint has alleged violations of the specific *Rules* indicated above. Though the complainant need not be a person directly harmed by the conduct in question, it is reasonable to assume that this particular complaint probably would have been brought by a former agent and/or former policyholder. It is likewise reasonable to assume that Joe President's decision did not violate any law or regulation. If not, there would be no further consideration of *R3.3,* and the inquiry would focus on whether any other ethics *Rule* had been violated.

Despite the fact that the members of the Board share with thousands of others a growing concern about the numerous social issues posed by the role of the automobile in our society, and despite the natural inclination to feel genuine compassion for the agents and policyholders involved in the case, the Board is not empowered to take disciplinary action unless and until a *Rule* has been violated. Nor will the Board allow itself to stretch the *Code* language in an effort to find a convenient scapegoat for social problems far beyond the ability of any one individual to solve. Thus, since the Board finds no evidence of any *Rule* violation, this case would be dismissed on its merits.

In reaching this conclusion, the Board sharply takes issue with Joe President's contention that his first and most important responsibility is to his stockholders. True, Joe President's occupational duties make him directly answerable to his Board of Directors and ultimately to the shareholders, and in this case it is probable that he complied with *R4.1* by competently discharging such duties. But his first and most important responsibility as a CPCU is his *ethical* responsibility to understand and abide by the *Rules* of professional conduct. Though his occupational duties would seldom, if ever, be in conflict with the *Rules*, his status as a CPCU makes him answerable to a higher authority should a conflict arise. Indeed, that is precisely what distinguishes professional from nonprofessional behavior. For example, it is entirely conceivable that a president could maximize the return to shareholders (at least in the short run) by initiating or condoning criminal or other unlawful activity. It is likewise conceivable that he could maximize short-run returns through conduct which is legal but prohibited under the *Code of Professional Ethics*. In either case, he would be subject to disciplinary action on ethics grounds.

What "excused" Joe President's conduct in this case was *not* that his "first responsibility is to his shareholders," but rather that he did not violate any ethics *Rules*. His decision to cancel the agency contracts was not "dishonest, deceitful, or fraudulent" (*R3.1*), and there is no evidence that Joe President failed to support the kinds of improvements called for in *R4.2* and *G4.2*. Some might argue that his decision was contrary to the aspirational goals of *Canon 1* (serving the public interest) and *Canon 3* (avoiding unjust harm to others). So also could it be argued that President failed to maintain dignified and honorable relationships with agents and policyholders (in accord with the spirit of *Canon 6*). Yet it could just as well be argued that the spirit of these three *Canons* would have been more seriously breached if the company had continued to do business in that state at the permitted rate levels and then become financially insolvent. However persuasive such arguments might be, they are not sufficient to support an ethics disciplinary action in the absence of a *Rule* violation.

The Board hopes that Joe President will join with all other insurance professionals in an earnest effort to find satisfactory solutions to the kinds of complex problems reflected in the case. In the meantime, without condoning Joe President's decision, the Board does not feel an ethics disciplinary action against Joe President would provide such a solution. Nor would it otherwise be justified under the Code.

CASE HCS-106

Ms. Polly Browne, CPCU, is director of advertising and public relations for a large insurer specializing in individual health insurance. Ms. Browne approved copy for various media advertisements which said "we will write health insurance for you even if you are sick or disabled or have been turned down by other insurers . . . In fact, we will write health insurance for anyone, regardless of age or health." A competitor insurer accuses Ms. Browne of *Code* violations because the ad did not specify that the insurance in question always contains a very restrictive exclusion for "preexisting conditions."

OPINION HCS-106

The Polly Browne Case could involve violations of laws or regulations governing deceptive advertising and thus, the application of *R3.3*. However, since the primary educational objective of the case is to clarify the extent to which the *Code* goes beyond the law, the *Opinion* will focus on the standards contained in *Rules R3.1, R7.2, Guidelines G3.1, G7.4*, and *Canons 3* and 7.

In the absence of evidence to the contrary, the Board would like to presume that Ms. Browne did not intend to defraud anyone. If not, the question which still remains is whether her approval of the advertising copy constituted an "omission of a dishonest or deceitful nature" (under *R3.1*) and/or a misrepresentation of the "limitations of . . . any product . . . of an insurer" (under *R7.2*). Though *G3.1* leaves the matter of how much information should be volunteered partially up to Ms. Browne's professional judgment, it also reminds her not to conceal facts which are material to determining the limitations of an insurance contract. And *G7.4* explicitly instructs her not to engage in deceptive advertising practices which significantly mislead the public. Taking all these standards together, and mindful of the spirit of *Canons 3* and 7, the Board feels Ms. Browne violated both of the applicable *Rules*. As a practical matter, advertising copy cannot be expected to list all of the exclusions and limitations of an insurance contract offered for sale. But in this case there can be little doubt that the public would be significantly misled by the failure to at least mention the preexisting conditions exclusion since the copy itself strongly suggests otherwise.

The Board would probably issue an informal admonition requesting Polly Browne to cease and desist, that is, to alter the advertising copy so as to conform to the letter and spirit of the *Code*. Stronger sanctions would be imposed only if she failed to comply with the Board's request. The Board believes that comparatively mild disciplinary action is appropriate in this case, but not because the advertising practice in question is fairly common in some segments of the industry. Instead, the action is an acknowledgment of the inherent difficulties posed by the very nature of advertising in contemporary society. If Company A is said to have "the best soap in the world," is this mere "puffery" or is it outright deception? To what extent should the consumer rely on representations made in advertising? To what extent should the consumer expect advertising to supply all the information needed to make a purchasing decision? That the courts and legislators have struggled with questions such as these is understandable. The issues are formidable in their own right, all the more so when the product is a necessarily complex legal contract like health insurance. Consequently, the Board sees no good reason to impose a harsh penalty on Polly Browne. Unless she blatantly disregards the Board's initial admonitions, it seems enough to remind her that her *Code* obligations require more than obedience to the letter of the law. The Board will not shrink from its responsibility to discipline *Rule* violators, but neither will it allow a preoccupation with discipline to obscure the larger goal of effecting voluntary compliance with the prescribed ethical norms.

CASE HCS-107

Charles Consultant, CPCU, operates his own small insurance consulting business solely in a state which does not require him to be licensed either as a consultant, agent, or broker. Mr. Consultant has extensive business insurance experience and is highly regarded by the corporate clients for whom he consults. He charges all consulting clients a fee of $100 per hour (plus expenses) for his services, which consist largely of drawing up bid specifications for various kinds of insurance, soliciting competitive bids, analyzing the bid proposals, and making recommendations to the client-buyer. Consultant does not recommend agents or brokers per se. Instead, he leaves it up to the buyer to decide whether he is to solicit bids from agents and brokers specified by the buyer or advertise openly for bids from any interested party. For one large corporate client, Mr. Consultant recommends that the client discontinue a particular insurance policy at its renewal date, replace it with aggregate and specific excess-of-loss coverage with large deductibles, and handle the underlying loss exposure with a carefully planned program of funded retention. He also recommends that the client study the feasibility of forming or acquiring its own captive insurer. A local agent alleges that Consultant is guilty of highly unethical conduct because "he always recommends self-insurance, his fees are too high, and he is not even a licensed agent or a member of the agents' association." A second agent objects to what he calls the "unfair competition of Consultant allowing only selected agents to bid for the better client-buyers." And a third agent challenges the ethics of "competitive bidding for private corporations and always recommending to them the lowest priced bid."

OPINION HCS-107

The standards which might apply most directly to the Charles Consultant case are those contained in *Rules R3.2, R4.1, R7.1, R7.2, Guidelines G3.3, G7.5,* and *Canons 3, 4,* and *7.* However, since there is no evidence that any *Rules* were violated by Consultant, the case would be dismissed on its merits.

Despite the unsupported allegations of the three local agents, the law does not require Consultant to be licensed or to join the agents' association, and there is nothing in his conduct, bidding procedures, or recommendations which would violate laws, regulations, or other standards in the ethics *Code.* To the contrary, Consultant appears to be competently and consistently discharging his duties in full compliance with *R4.1.* Recommendations concerning deductibles, funded retention, and the feasibility of captive insurers may even be ethically required in given factual situations where they best serve the client's interests, by the dictates of *Rules R7.1, R7.2,* and *G7.5.* Such recommendations are certainly not ipso facto unethical in the present case. If Consultant always recommended self-insurance and/or the lowest priced bid, as was alleged, it would raise questions about both his competence and his ethics. But the Board finds no evidence to support these allegations.

Nor does the Board see anything unethical about the size of Consultant's hourly fee. We assume that the employer-clients agreed in advance to pay Consultant $100 per hour for agreed-upon services, and that he actually delivered those services. Thus, whether the fee was $100 or $1,000 per hour, it was neither "at the expense of the uninformed" nor "unconscionable" within the meaning of G3.3, nor did it violate R3.2, because the evidence suggests that Consultant's recommendations were in the best interests of his clients. He did not allow the pursuit of financial gain to interfere with the exercise of his sound professional judgment and skills.

The Board will not apply R3.2 to sit in judgment of the level of compensation a CPCU receives in the marketplace for his or her services since it is not the absolute level of compensation which makes professional services ethically suspect. It is whether the pursuit of any amount of financial gain clouded the judgment of the professional, that is, seduced him to make judgments which were not in the best interests of those served, that makes professional services suspect. The purpose of R3.2 is to prohibit the CPCU from doing something analogous to the surgeon who, in pursuit of a fee, performs surgery that is neither necessary nor desirable for the patient. The surgeon's professional peers would undoubtedly regard his conduct as unethical, whether the fee was $50 or $5,000 because it was the act of performing the surgery that was unethical. The fee was merely the inducement.

CASE HCS-108

John Johnson, CPCU, has been a casualty underwriter for thirty-five years. He received his designation in 1958 when he was enthusiastic about insurance education and felt that the designation would help him in his climb up the corporate ladder. Having been locked in to a dead-end job for the past five years with no hope of breaking out, his attitude toward continuing education has changed. He has dropped out of a local CPCU chapter, refuses to attend meetings of any kind, discourages fellow employees from seeking the designation, and is simply awaiting retirement. His job performance is acceptable in every respect. He has not signed an election to be bound by the *Rules* of the *Code*. Nevertheless, the president of the local CPCU chapter requests that the Board of Ethical Inquiry take appropriate action under *R2.1* and *R5.2*.

OPINION HCS-108

The case of John Johnson would have to be dismissed for lack of jurisdiction. Since Johnson received his CPCU designation prior to July 1976, and since he did not file a voluntary written election to be bound by the *Rules*, the Board has no authority to take any disciplinary action against him (as specified in the *Preamble* and reaffirmed in *Opinion HCS-102*).

Had Johnson been subject to the binding effect of the *Rules*, he would probably be disciplined by admonishment, reprimand, or even censure for clear-cut violations of *R5.2*. That *Rule* would not obligate him to encourage everyone to pursue CPCU studies, but it would obligate him to encourage and assist *those who wish to pursue* CPCU or other studies, in keeping with the spirit of *Canon 5*. Johnson's attitude toward continuing education would also justify a determination of whether he had violated his own continuing education obligation under *R2.1* and the related *Guidelines*.

CASE HCS-109

Jack Fieldman, CPCU, a field representative of a small multiline insurer, is making a sales presentation with an agent who is not a CPCU. Acquiring the account would greatly enhance Jack's position with his company because it is a prestigious account and a sales campaign is in progress. Part of the proposal is a business package policy with a $1,000 deductible applicable to the property coverages.

In his zeal to make the sale, Jack fails to disclose the deductible. He feels no guilt because he knows that many of his competitors do not mention deductibles unless specifically asked by the applicant or insured.

If a complaint is received from the insured, should any disciplinary action be taken against Fieldman?

OPINION HCS-109

The standards most directly applicable to the Jack Fieldman Case are those contained in *Rules R3.1* and *R7.2, Guidelines G3.1*, and *Canons 3* and *7*.

Since it does not appear that Fieldman was guilty of a misrepresentation within the meaning of *R7.2*, the issue turns on whether his failure to disclose a policy provision constituted a violation of *R3.1*. Specifically, was his nondisclosure an "omission of a dishonest, deceitful, or fraudulent nature?"

Guideline G3.1 illustrates the general kinds of acts and omissions which can violate R3.1, and which normally "would cause unjust harm to others," thus violating the spirit of Canon 3. The Guideline explicitly stipulates, "A CPCU should neither misrepresent nor conceal a fact or information which is material to determining the . . . scope or *limitations* of an insurance contract" [emphasis supplied]. However, the *Guideline* goes on to say, ". . . the extent to which a CPCU should volunteer information and facts must necessarily be left to sound professional judgment of what is required under the circumstances."

Clearly, the drafters of the *Code* did not intend to treat every omission as though it were dishonest, deceitful, or fraudulent if only because it would be so obviously unrealistic to require CPCUs to give every prospective purchaser a full-scale educational course on every insurance contract under consideration. But it also seems clear, from all the relevant standards taken together, that an omission would violate *R3.1* if, based on sound professional judgment, the voluntary disclosure of facts or information is required by the circumstances because the disclosure is (1) material to the buyer's decision making and (2) necessary to avoid what would otherwise cause unjust harm to others.

This type of nondisclosure may be common among his competitors, as Jack contends, but his ethical obligations are prescribed by the *Code* and not by the conduct of others. The Board believes Jack Fieldman did violate *R3.1*, that he was aware of his ethical obligations under the *Rule*, and that he felt himself to be excused by the practices of others (many of whom are not subject to the *Code*). The Board would at least issue a private admonition requesting Fieldman to cease and desist, and the disciplinary penalty might be more severe if there was sufficient evidence of fraud and/or if the insured had been significantly harmed. In any event, the insured would be reminded that the Board's action under the *Code* is independent of any remedies the insured may have at law.

CASE HCS-110

Ann Underwriter, CPCU, is an auto underwriter with the Fire and Casualty Company. Her job includes the selection and rejection of applicants for auto insurance and requires that she make a decision regarding the class into which the applicant will be placed. All applicants are categorized as above average, or below average, and the premium charged is considerably higher for below average insureds.

One of the agents in her territory is Sue Agent, who also runs a foreign car agency. Sue's business is dominated by members of one ethnic group who live in a section of the city that is somewhat rundown, but there are no available data to indicate a higher-than-average loss ratio in that area. Ann has automatically classed these applicants as below average because she believes that they are bad risks. Has Ann violated the ethics *Code?*

OPINION HCS-110

In most jurisdictions, underwriting practices predicated upon the ethnic origin of the applicant (or insured) would be unlawful discrimination under applicable state and federal statutes and regulations. Therefore, the practice of Ann Underwriter would likewise be a violation of *R3.3* under the *Code*, and she would be subject to disciplinary action. If she attempted to plead ignorance of the applicable law, she would be acknowledging that she also violated *R2.1* and *R6.1*. An underwriter who is not familiar with antidiscrimination laws is violating her duty to "keep informed on those technical matters that are essential to the maintenance of [her] professional competence," as well as her duty to "keep informed on the legal limitations imposed upon the scope of . . . professional activities."

Assuming Ann Underwriter did violate one or more *Rules*, she would at least be issued an informal admonition to cease and desist. And she would be forewarned that any additional *Rule* violation will subject her to the possibility of more severe penalties.

If Ann Underwriter did not in fact violate any law or regulation, on the other hand, the case would be dismissed on its merits. Perhaps her conduct would have been contrary to the spirit of several *Canons* and *Guidelines*, but it would not have breached any *Rule*. The drafters of the *Code* chose not to include an ethics *Rule* on discrimination per se in recognition of the fact that the very process of pooling involves certain types of lawful discrimination as an actuarial necessity, and certain types of discrimination are also required by law as a matter of rating equity. Thus, a CPCU will not be guilty of an ethics violation for discrimination unless (1) it is unlawful discrimination (which would be a breach of *R3.3*) or (2) the discrimination itself is lawful but otherwise involves an act or omission prohibited by the *Rules*.

CASE HCS-111

A CPCU who is a loss prevention engineer employed by an insurance company feels that an insured firm is engaging in practices which violate many of the requirements of the Occupational Safety and Health Act. The CPCU reports these violations to the insurer's underwriting department but not to the Occupational Safety and Health Administration (OSHA).

To what extent, if any, is the CPCU subject to discipline under the *Code?*

OPINION HCS-111

Under certain circumstances, the engineer case might involve violations of laws or regulations (and thus, the application of *R3.3* as well as related Rules and *Guidelines*). However, in keeping with the educational objective of the case, the Opinion will focus on the standards contained in *Rules R4.1, R5.4, R6.2, R7.2, Guidelines G4.7, G6.6, G7.2,* and *Canons* 6 and 7.

We will assume that a proper complaint has been brought and that Engineer is subject to the binding effect of the *Rules.* It is also reasonable to assume that Engineer informed the insured firm of the practices which he felt were not in compliance with OSHA, in which case Engineer did not violate *R7.2* or the spirit of *G7.2* and *Canon 7.* Had Engineer represented that the firm was in full compliance with OSHA, he would have violated *R3.1* (by committing, in the conduct of his professional activities, an act of a dishonest nature). In fact, even if the firm appeared to be in full compliance with OSHA, Engineer should make clear to the insured firm that this is merely a professional opinion; otherwise, he would run the danger of violating *R7.2* ("A CPCU shall not misrepresent the . . . limitations or any . . . service of an insurer.")

By disclosing this information to his underwriting department, Engineer did not violate *R6.2* since such disclosure is specifically permitted when "made to a person who necessarily must have the information in order to discharge legitimate occupational or professional duties." Indeed, in this case, Engineer's disclosure to underwriting is consistent with his *R4.1* duty to "competently... discharge [his own] occupational duties." Furthermore, Engineer's failure to report the firm's practices to OSHA does not violate *R5.4.* The latter *Rule* does not obligate him to volunteer information. It only obligates him to disclose information *officially requested by appropriate regulatory authorities,* and then only regarding laws governing the qualifications or conduct of *insurance practitioners.*

Since we have assumed that no law or regulation was violated by Engineer, and since no other *Rules* of the *Code* were breached, the case would be dismissed on its merits.

CASE HCS-112

A CPCU who is a full-time risk manager regularly renews his employer's insurance with the same insurers year after year, refusing insurance agents' requests for specifications to be used for competitive bids. The CPCU's refusal is based on an honest, but mistaken, belief that the insurance that the company now carries provides the best available coverage and claim service at the lowest available cost. No complaint has been filed with the Board of Ethical Inquiry (BEI).

Is this CPCU subject to discipline for violation of the *Code?* May the agent, who is a CPCU candidate, call the matter to the attention of the Board of Ethical Inquiry? If so, what are the required procedures?

OPINION HCS-112

To clarify the procedural question, suppose a member of the BEI read in the newspaper about a person who had been indicted for embezzlement. The member just happened to know that the indicted person is a CPCU. This kind of situation obviously would prompt an investigation at the Board's own initiative. However, the Board is usually not aware of an alleged *Code* violation unless and until someone voluntarily reports it to the Ethics Counsel. Any person may report an alleged violation. So also may any person file a formal complaint as long as the complaint is in compliance with the American Institute's published *Disciplinary Rules and Procedures.*

In the Risk Manager Case, let us suppose that the agent reported an alleged *Rule* violation. Unless the agent signed a written complaint, or his informal oral report prompted an investigation which later revealed sufficient evidence of a possible *Rule* violation, the case would be dismissed as frivolous and prima facie without merit. Thus, to preserve the educational value of the case, we will assume that Risk Manager has been appropriately accused of violating *Rule R4.1* and the spirit of *Canon 4.*

Rule R4.1 stipulates, "A CPCU shall competently and consistently discharge his or her occupational duties." Nonetheless, *Guideline G4.1* makes it clear that ". . . the Board will not intervene nor arbitrate between the parties in an employment or contractual relationship . . . Nor does the Board feel that the Institute's disciplinary procedures should become a substitute for legal and other remedies available to such parties. In the event of an alleged violation of *Rule R4.1,* therefore, the Board will hear the case only after all other remedies have been exhausted. . . ." As an employee, Risk Manager has an employment relationship with his employer-firm. His employer is the primary party to whom his occupational duties are owed. If the risk manager is guilty of failing to discharge his occupational duties competently and consistently, the employer may dismiss him and/or take other appropriate actions. If no such actions are taken by the employer or other affected parties (for example, the stockholders), the BEI will not hear the case.

Furthermore, *G4.1* goes on to say that, even when all other remedies have been exhausted, the Board will take disciplinary action "only under circumstances where (1) a proven violation has caused unjust harm to another *person* and the violation brings substantial discredit upon the CPCU designation; or (2) it would otherwise be in the *public* interest to take disciplinary action under the ethics code" [emphasis supplied]. Since there is no evidence that either of these two criteria are met in the hypothetical case, the Board would not take disciplinary action under *R4.1*. By renewing his firm's insurance with the same insurers year after year, the risk manager may be acting with admirable competence, particularly under tight market conditions. Or, the facts may reveal a human error in judgment, an error of the type which even the most competent professional can make, which would not in itself violate the *Rule*. Even if the facts support a finding of incompetence on the part of Risk Manager, the other (*G4.1*) prerequisites of disciplinary action are not met in this case. The only basis of disciplinary action against Risk Manager is that he may have violated *R2.1* (that is, he may have failed to keep informed on those matters which are essential to the maintenance of his professional competence as a risk manager). As indicated in *G2.3*, "if a CPCU is accused of violating any other *Rule* in the *Code*, the Board may, at its discretion, require the accused to furnish evidence of compliance with *Rule 2.1*." Such evidence of compliance is especially likely to be sought in cases involving allegations of incompetence.

Finally, it should be noted that the rationale of *G4.1* is not limited to cases involving the employer-employee relationship per se. It applies to *any* alleged violation of *R4.1*, that is, to any case where a CPCU (or CPCU candidate) is accused of failing to discharge his or her occupational duties competently and consistently. The Board will not hear the case unless and until all other available remedies have been exhausted.

CASE HCS-113

A CPCU who is an agent is negotiating manuscript products liability coverage with an insurance company underwriter. He doubts that the underwriter is aware that the Consumer Product Safety Commission (CPSC) is considering investigating the safety of one of his client's products. An unfavorable finding by the Commission is likely to force the client-company to incur large product recall expenses, which will be covered by the policy being negotiated if it is issued. The agent does not mention to the underwriter this possible action by the Commission, and the underwriter does not ask about any such action.

To what extent, if any, is this CPCU subject to discipline under the *Code?* If the CPCU was a broker instead of an agent, would this be material to the findings of the Board?

OPINION HCS-113

While it is true that Agent has a contractual relationship with his insurer-principal, we assume he was not accused of violating *R4.1;* hence, the Board may hear the case, apart from any remedies which may be available to the insurer.

The real issue here is whether Agent violated his *R3.1* duty by engaging in "any act or omission of a dishonest, deceitful, or fraudulent nature." Generally speaking, since underwriting techniques and requirements vary considerably among insurers, the Board believes it would be unreasonable to expect an agent to know every kind of information a particular underwriter would deem material to the writing of a particular kind of insurance. Thus, the Board sees no ethical reason for an agent to volunteer information in his possession *except* when (1) the information is specifically requested in the application, (2) the information is specifically requested by the underwriter or other authorized employee of the insurer, OR (3) the agent knows that the information is material to most insurers writing the kind of insurance in question, and the agent has good reason to believe the insurer cannot readily discover the information through inspection or other commonly used sources of underwriting information. (That he should know these things is reinforced by *R2.1.*) As indicated in G3.1, "the extent to which a CPCU should volunteer information and facts must necessarily be left to sound professional judgment of what is required under the circumstances." The above three criteria are provided to assist agent-CPCUs in making sound professional judgments about the disclosure of information to underwriters.

In this case, Agent surely knew that a pending CPSC investigation would be material to any of the few insurers who write products recall coverage, that is, he at least should have known that the information might well affect the insurer's underwriting decision or the pricing of the insurance. He, therefore, was guilty of concealing a material fact, ethically if not legally.

He violated *R3.1* by engaging in an omission of a dishonest or deceitful nature (whether the omission was also fraudulent would depend on his intent). In the absence of evidence to the contrary, it can be inferred that he also might have violated *R3.2* by allowing "the pursuit of financial gain . . . to interfere with the exercise of sound professional judgment and skills." The Board would reprimand the agent in the form of an informal rebuke given limited publication. If there was satisfactory evidence of fraud, the Board would recommend public censure or suspension of the privilege to use the CPCU designation, and the final decision would be made by the Ethics Policy Committee of the American Institute's Board of Trustees.

The same conclusion would essentially be reached if the accused had been a broker instead of an agent. True, in most states an agent is legally a representative of the insurer, whereas the broker is a representative of the applicant or insured. The legal duties of the two may differ somewhat. But the ethical duties under the *Code* do not. Both have ethical duties to their clients, and both are summoned by *Canon 1* to put the public interest above their own. *Guideline G1.2* acknowledges apparent or real conflicts of interest. Yet, it also reminds us that the *public* interest is best served by strict compliance to the prescribed *Rules* of ethical conduct. We cannot believe that an agent's knowing concealment from an insurer of a material fact is in the public interest. And the ethics of any act or omission remain the same whether or not the action is committed by a broker or an agent.

CASE HCS-114

A CPCU who is a risk manager has purchased for his firm, in the nonadmitted market, an insurance coverage which the risk manager knows is available in the admitted market, but at a higher premium than the nonadmitted coverage. The CPCU knows that the broker through whom the nonadmitted coverage was purchased did not comply with the applicable surplus lines law. Has the risk manager violated any *Rules* under the *Code?*

OPINION HCS-114

Though most surplus lines laws contain a number of specific exemptions which might excuse the conduct of the broker and the risk manager, the Board will assume as fact that the broker did violate the applicable law. The Board has no jurisdiction over the broker since he is not a CPCU or CPCU candidate. The question is whether the CPCU risk manager has violated any *Rules* of the ethics *Code*.

Despite the fact that the risk manager did not directly violate a law or regulation (and therefore is not subject to discipline under R3.3), he did violate his R1.2 duty. He may not literally have advocated or sanctioned the broker's conduct. But he did "otherwise carry out through another or condone" an act (violating the law) which he himself is prohibited from performing by the *Rules* of the ethics *Code*. The risk manager would be informally admonished for unethical conduct and given a reasonable length of time to make satisfactory insurance arrangements for his firm. In some states, for example, he might be able to obtain the Commissioner's approval of an arrangement which would, in the absence of such approval, violate the surplus lines law. If he could not do so, he would be ethically obligated to place the insurance with an authorized insurer, even if it meant higher premiums for his employer firm because that is what is required by the typical law. A particular law may appear to be unreasonable or unfair, but that does not leave a CPCU free to violate it, either directly or through another. Nor does the fact that a law penalizes his employer excuse a CPCU for violating *R1.2* of the *Code*. A CPCU's first ethical obligation is to serve the public interest by strict compliance with all the *Code Rules* (see G1.2).

The risk manager would not be obligated by *R5.4* to report the broker's law violation unless the risk manager had been properly subpoenaed by the appropriate regulatory authorities in the process of investigating or prosecuting the broker's alleged violation of the insurance laws. In fact, as a practical matter, this particular case might never be brought to the attention of the Board of Ethical Inquiry. It is conceivable that a Commissioner or an authorized insurer would be willing to register an ethics complaint. But the broker or employer-policyholder surely would not. The case is no less valuable as an educational tool, nonetheless, in keeping with the Board's desire to foster and encourage voluntary compliance with the prescribed ethical norms. Furthermore, suppose a case with essentially the same facts involved two CPCUs who are brokers in competition for the risk manager's account, and assume that one broker had secured the account with a lower premium proposal from an unauthorized insurer, in violation of the surplus lines law. Realistically, a competitor broker, having been harmed, is more likely to file an ethics complaint with the Board.

CASE HCS-115

John Manager, CPA, CPCU, is the treasurer of a large insurance company. In order to induce Brown, a potential investor, to purchase a substantial portion of its new bond issue, Manager intentionally certified the financial status of XYZ Corporation, the manufacturer of firefighting equipment, as sound. In fact, Manager knew the XYZ Corporation was nearly insolvent, but he was persuaded to do so by his brother-in-law, the president of XYZ Corporation, in the honest belief that without the successful sale of the bond issue several hundred employees of XYZ would lose their jobs.

After the bonds had been purchased by Brown, the scheme was discovered and Manager, in addition to criminal penalties, was disciplined by the State Institute of Certified Public Accountants.

Is Manager subject to disciplinary action under the CPCU ethics *Code* if it can be shown by proper evidence that:

   (a) he personally and financially benefited from his illegal act?
       OR
   (b) he was solely motivated by his concern for the jobs involved and no one has sustained any loss in consequence of his act?
       OR
   (c) XYZ Corporation was not a manufacturer, but a large insurance brokerage firm; otherwise, the facts are the same as in (b)?

OPINION HCS-115

It is quite clear that John Manager violated his R3.1 duty by engaging in an "act or omission of a dishonest, deceitful or fraudulent nature." Since this *Rule* applies to any "business or professional activities," it would not matter that the XYZ Corporation was an insurance brokerage firm or a manufacturer, as asked in hypothetical question (c). It is a *Rule* violation in either case.

Manager also violated the security laws. He is therefore subject to disciplinary action under *R3.3*, as further clarified under *G3.4*. If Manager financially benefited from his act, as suggested in hypothetical question (a), he also violated *R3.2* (by allowing the pursuit of financial gain to interfere with the exercise of sound professional judgments and skills). In view of the criminal conviction, the Board would immediately suspend the privilege to use the CPCU designation. If the Ethics Policy Committee concurred with the recommendation, the suspension would remain in effect until such time that Manager could provide convincing proof of full and complete rehabilitation.

Hypothetical question (b) slightly changes the circumstances by assuming that Manager was motivated solely by an altruistic concern for the employees and that no one sustained any loss as a consequence of his act. His motivations do not alter the conclusion that he violated *Rules* of the *Code*. When criminal conviction is not involved, a violator's motivations may be taken into consideration, along with other factors, in determining the severity of the penalty to be imposed.

CASE HCS-116

A CPCU making calls in a community is reviewing an insurance portfolio with a prospective new client (a gas station operator) and finds a garage liability policy that expired forty-five days ago. With it is a thirty-day binder and a cover letter from the present agent saying that the renewal policy should be mailed within ten days. Nothing has been received in the interim. The new agent says, "The cold, hard facts are that you have no proof of coverage at all, and if you were sued because of an injury here on the premises or arising out of the operation of your car or wrecker, you might find yourself high and dry. This isn't to say that you couldn't eventually recover the damages from the insurance company or the agent, but it might be very difficult for you to do it—and it might cost you a lot in terms of time and legal expense. It appears that your agent has mishandled your account, and I recommend that you get new coverage into effect immediately. I can leave a written binder with you right now and will have the new policy back here within ten days." The gas station operator said, "OK, let's do it!" The former agent learned of this discussion two weeks later when he delivered the "renewal policy." He now contends that the CPCU's action was unethical and that the situation demanded a telephone call to find out whether a current binder was in effect. A formal complaint is filed with the Ethics Counsel of the Institute, after which it becomes known that a member of the Board of Ethical Inquiry is a competitor of the CPCU being charged with an ethics violation. The CPCU being charged lives over 2,000 miles from Malvern, PA.

OPINION HCS-116

The CPCU's conversation with a client suggests the possibility that a competitor may eventually bring a legal action for slanderous defamation of character, which would be a matter for the courts to decide. There also might be a basis for contending that the CPCU's conduct was contrary to the spirit of *Canon* 6 and *Guidelines* G6.1 and G6.2 (which summon a CPCU to strive for dignified and honorable relationships with competitors). Against this it can be argued that his conduct did not cause "*unjust* harm to others" within the meaning of *Canon* 3. Vigorous competition is often in the public interest, and it is not inherently unethical to offer improvements in a prospective client's insurance arrangements. Indeed, an agent who did not do so ordinarily would be violating his *R4.1* obligation to discharge his occupational duties competently. A dignified and honorable professional does not make a habit of criticizing his competitors in a personal manner. Yet, whenever an insurance advisor convinces a client of the need to effect improvements in existing insurance arrangements, a need which is not infrequent, there is nothing to keep the client from drawing the inference that his previous advisors were careless or incompetent. Clearly, a client can benefit from a particular agent's knowledge, skill, and diligence. And the Board sees no ethical reason why such an agent should be required to telephone or otherwise share with his competitor a lawful and desirable trade advantage which he has obtained through his own efforts. Whatever the merits of these arguments may be, the Board is not empowered to take disciplinary action unless a *Rule* of the *Code* has been violated.

Given the brief description of the hypothetical case, about the only *Rule* which might be applicable is R3.1 (which imposes a duty to refrain from allowing the pursuit of financial gain to interfere with the exercise of sound professional judgment), and it should be interpreted within the context of *Canon 3*. The CPCU's use of phrases like "mishandled your account" borders on the indiscreet. But the Board finds no persuasive evidence of unsound professional judgment which would cause unjust harm to others. Accordingly, the case would be dismissed on its merits.

If the case had progressed to the stage of a hearing, the initial hearing would be held in the geographical proximity of the accused so as to minimize travel expenses. And a member of the BEI is obligated to disqualify himself or herself if serving on the hearing panel would involve a potential conflict of interest (for example, serving as a judge of a competitor).

CASE HCS-117

A CPCU who is a part-time university professor decided to run a Saturday morning CPCU 1 class from 8:00 a.m. to noon on the first Saturday in the month. When the local chapter people heard of the plan, they contacted him to discuss two aspects of such a plan:

1. the educational feasibility of his plan to present all material through lectures and handout materials he prepared, without requiring students to study the textbook;

2. the fact that it would be in competition with their own plans for CPCU 1 on Tuesday evenings.

The professor dismissed the first point of discussion by noting that he had previously run a Naval Reserve Class, "Confidential Document Classification," on exactly the same basis and that it had been very successful. If it could work there, it certainly could work with CPCU. On the second point, he was confident that the people he would get on Saturday morning would be persons who would not be coming to the Tuesday night class anyway since "agents are always out making calls in the evening."

The chapter people called the Institute to see what could be done about the situation. An Institute staff member called the professor to discuss the potential educational pitfalls in the lecture-and-handout approach and told him of unsuccessful efforts in that direction in other communities. Professor indicated that since he already had thirty students who had submitted their $200, he felt obligated to proceed with the plan. Contact with the professor through the year revealed that the chapter/Institute predictions of attrition, nonpreparation, no exam practice, and so on, were being fulfilled as early as the November and December meetings. At the end of the year the roster sheet report to the professor revealed a course effectiveness ratio that was approximately one-third that of the national average. Concurrent with the receipt of the roster sheet feedback, the chapter president called again to say that a mailing had gone out again announcing another CPCU 1 class offering on the same basis. Their call to the professor led to his statement that "while there had been some problems with the group, I don't see any justification for concluding that it was the format that was the problem."

Yet another conversation with the professor was held by conference call with two Institute staff members, but the professor was not to be dissuaded. The fee had gone to $250 and the professor felt that there was a real interest and demand for this program on the part of the agents. Consequently, the professor was going to meet that need. The second year proceeded exactly the same as the first with almost identical results. At this point the chapter president contacted the professor in mid-June to find out what his plans were. When he said that he was going to reoffer this course, the chapter president asked for Institute assistance through involvement of the Board of Ethical Inquiry.

OPINION HCS-117

The Board notes with regret the lack of the professor's cooperation with the local CPCU chapter, as well as the unfortunate educational results of his efforts. However, it should also be acknowledged that the American Institute does not *require* any particular method of preparing for the national CPCU examinations. Students and instructors alike are encouraged to follow the educational advice of qualified Institute staff members, and students are offered a free program of individualized counseling. Yet, it is a well-known fact that some CPCU students do not follow sound educational advice. Some continue to rely on "cram courses" and other shortcuts which the American Institute staff members feel are of questionable educational value. But the American Institute's examination requirements do not *prohibit* participation in such courses, either as an instructor or a student. Nor would an instructor who did so violate any law. Thus, the issue in the hypothetical case is whether the professor's approach is otherwise unethical under the *Code*.

Unless a chapter member or other person was willing to file a formal complaint against the professor, the case would be dismissed as frivolous and prima facie without merit. Even a complaint would likewise be dismissed unless there was satisfactory evidence of a *Rule* violation. If a complaint was filed in this case, it would probably allege violations of *R6.3*, *R4.1*, and *R3.2*. Let us briefly consider each.

Rule 6.3 stipulates that a "CPCU shall not knowingly misrepresent or conceal any limitations on the CPCU's ability to provide the . . . quality of professional services required by the circumstances." It would be difficult for an instructor to conceal the general results of his previous CPCU classes. The Institute releases to CPCU chapters the names of the area candidates who successfully passed one or more national examinations. The local people can at least compare the list with the number of persons who initially enrolled in a particular class (and they can sometimes determine who actually sat for a particular exam). The professor could have violated the *Rule* by misrepresenting the quality of services he would provide especially if he led students to believe he would guarantee that they would pass the national examination. But there is no evidence of the latter in the description of the case.

The criteria of *G4.1* would seem to be met well enough for the Board to hear an allegation of incompetence under *R4.1*. Nonetheless, the application of the *Rule* is a bit clouded by the fact that most CPCU instructors are part-time volunteers whose primary occupational duties are owed to employers or clients. More important, evaluating the competence of an instructor is an inherently difficult task. It is done satisfactorily by some educational institutions, but it would be unfair for the Board to evaluate the ethics of CPCU instructors according to the American Institute's criteria for course effectiveness, since (1) CPCU instructors are not employed by the American Institute, (2) professional educators do not agree on all of the criteria and methods that should be used to evaluate teaching competence, and (3) there are a number of variables which effect the results of a learning opportunity, including the motivation, background, and efforts of the students themselves. Consequently, the Board cannot find, in *R4.1*, any clear-cut basis for disciplining an instructor on ethics grounds. (An instructor could of course be disciplined under *R2.1*, just like any other CPCU, but there is no evidence that this professor breached his continuing education duty.) If the local CPCU chapter employs an instructor, as is often the case, the chapter may use whatever instructor evaluation criteria and methods it chooses.

Finally, there is the question of whether the professor violated his *R3.2* duty by "allowing the pursuit of financial gain . . . to interfere with the exercise of sound professional judgment and skills." As spelled out in *Opinion HCS-107*, the Board will not apply *R3.2* to sit in judgment of the level of compensation a CPCU receives in the marketplace for his or her services since it is not the absolute level of compensation which makes professional services ethically suspect. It is whether the pursuit of any size financial gain clouded the judgment of the professional, that is, seduced him to make judgments which were not in the best interests of those served. Whether the students were unjustly harmed by this professor's financially induced and unsound professional judgment is a question of fact which cannot be determined based solely on the information given. If the facts supported such a finding, the professor would be informally admonished to cease and desist. If he did not heed the warning, the Board would reprimand him and recommend his public censure.

CASE HCS-118

Bernard Forman, CPCU, Assistant Manager of a regional office of the Old Line Insurance Company, had been working with one of the Casualty Department underwriters in an attempt to help one of the company's contractor-insureds obtain a sizable government contract. In the negotiation stage on insurance costs, there was a disagreement between Bernie and the underwriter over the amount to charge for coverage under the manuscript policy. The underwriter felt the account merited a $25,000 annual premium charge, but Bernie felt $2,000 was enough. The premium level would affect the bid and thus would be a determining factor in whether or not the contractor gets the job. Bernie told the underwriter that he was making an executive decision to charge only $2,000. The project was awarded to the contractor.

Two months after this experience, the underwriter found out that Bernie was a silent partner in the agency which handled the contractor's account. He feels that Bernie should remove himself from all further business decisions involving the agency, and he has requested the Board of Ethical Inquiry to take action on the specific case outlined. In order to substantiate the reasonableness of his $2,000 charge, Bernie cites the fact that the job was completed without any losses.

OPINION HCS-118

The purpose of including the Forman Case is to clarify the application of *R4.1* and *R3.1* to a specific conflict of interest situation. As an employee, Forman has an occupational duty of loyalty to his employer. He cannot discharge that duty consistently unless he is consistently honest about matters which may affect his employer. It therefore follows that Forman's failure to disclose his role as a silent partner is a violation of his *R4.1* duty under the ethics *Code*. However, G4.1 stipulates that the Board will not hear the matter of an alleged violation of *R4.1* until all other remedies have been exhausted. Assuming the employer discovered Forman's failure to disclose his interest in the agency, the employer might well be content to dismiss Forman and/or to take other actions without bringing an ethics complaint to the Board.

Apart from the employer's decision, the underwriter or any other person could file an ethics complaint which alleged violation of *R3.2* and *R3.1*. Forman may have been motivated by the pursuit of financial gain, but it would be very difficult to prove that he violated his *R3.2* duty because the determination of an adequate premium for manuscript coverages leaves ample room for substantial disagreements in judgment. The application of *R3.1* is another matter entirely. And the Board does feel that Forman's failure to disclose (to his employer) his agency partnership role is an "omission of a dishonest or deceit-

ful nature" within the meaning of *R3.1*. Accordingly, the Board would reprimand Forman and forewarn him of the more severe penalties which might
follow an additional Rule violation.

CASE HCS-119

Bill Executive, CPCU, is a manager of a large branch office of a national insurance company. He often entertains his neighbors and friends and charges the expenses off to his company. His expense accounts reflect that he entertained agents. When he wants to show his appreciation to his office employees for one reason or another, he advises them to take their spouses out for an evening on the town and show it on their expense accounts as entertaining agents.

John Candidate, a young underwriter studying CPCU 5, has received permission from Bill to take Mrs. Candidate out to dinner and charge it to the company. Permission was granted because John was able to get Bill a discount on a new color TV.

Because John has real reservations about the proposed method of handling personal entertainment expenses, he has written to the Board of Ethical Inquiry to determine whether this sort of conduct would be a breach of the *Code* by Bill or himself.

OPINION HCS-119

The Bill Executive-John Candidate Case has two primary educational objectives. The first is to remind readers that John Candidate's inquiry would be promptly answered by the Ethics Counsel. Candidate would be commended for observing the spirit of the *G1.2* concept which says: "When there is good reason for a person subject to the Code to be uncertain as to the ethical propriety of a specific activity or type of conduct, that person should refrain from engaging in such activity or conduct until the matter has been clarified. Any CPCU or CPCU candidate who needs assistance in interpreting the *Code* is encouraged to request an advisory opinion from the American Institute's Board of Ethical Inquiry." John Candidate would be issued an advisory opinion, and it would later be published, with names changed to conceal identities, if it was of general import.

The second objective of the case is to address the sometimes troublesome matter of expense accounts. *R3.3* makes it clear that a CPCU will be subject to disciplinary action for the violation of any law or regulation relating to professional activities. The *Rule* most certainly includes violations of IRS regulations as well as violations of the Internal Revenue Code (and comparable state laws and regulations).

If Bill Executive and John Candidate are complying with the tax laws, and if their employer has given Bill Executive a free hand to reward employees with generous expense account allowances, the Board sees nothing unethical about the activity of either Executive or Candidate. Yet, the description of the hypothetical case strongly suggests that Executive is running afoul of *R3.1* by engaging in "any act or omission of a dishonest, deceitful, or fraudulent nature." It appears that he may also be violating the applicable tax laws and regulations. If so, and if a proper complaint were to be filed, Executive would be severely reprimanded by the Board, and harsher penalties would be considered. The conduct of Executive is not excused by any contention, however accurate, that "thousands of people cheat on their expense accounts." And Candidate would be forewarned that any complicity on his part would be considered participating in or condoning a prohibited act within the meaning of *R1.2*. If he is actually convicted of a crime, the Board would immediately suspend his right to use the CPCU designation.

There is one final point well worth mentioning. Because the Board earnestly wishes to encourage CPCUs and CPCU candidates to request advisory opinions, they are advised to use fictitious names in making such requests. Whether they wish later to report an alleged violation or file a complaint is left to their own discretion.

CASE HCS-120

J. R. "Pinky" Smith, CPCU, is an insurance agent in a small town. He starts a promotional campaign which includes a giveaway to clients and potential clients: a pen that reads: "'Pinky' Smith, CPCU, 25 years as an insurance professional, 1-800-555-5555." Tom Jackson, CPCU, the only other insurance agent in town, writes to the Institute complaining of Smith's promotional effort. Jackson requests the Institute to direct Smith to cease and desist. Should Smith be disciplined for violating *R8.1?*

OPINION HCS-120

Since *R8.1* incorporates by reference the *G8.1 Guidelines,* the latter have the binding effect of *Rules.* These *Guidelines* have the broad purpose of preventing the undignified and unprofessional use of the CPCU designation and the CPCU key.

Subparagraph a.3 of *Guideline* G8.1 states that the designation, initials, and key may not be affixed to any object, product, or property. Smith's use of the "CPCU" letters on a pen clearly violates this *Guideline.* It should be noted that subparagraph e of this *Guideline* allows the American Institute to grant exceptions. Any CPCU who contemplates a use of the designation, initials, or key that he or she believes is dignified and professional but that has not been explicitly authorized, may contact the Ethics Counsel to seek approval.

Whenever the Board feels a particular use is in violation of the *Code,* it will first request the violator to cease and desist. Additional penalties will be imposed only if the violator does not comply with the initial request. (Where an unauthorized person is using the designation, the failure to cease and desist will prompt the Institute to bring a legal action.)

CASE HCS-121

A member of the Board of Ethical Inquiry, while driving to work, hears the voice of an enchantress on his car radio: "No-sweat insurance—that's what you need . . . noooooo sweat . . . turn your insurance worries over to an insurance professional—let him sweat it for you . . . call Jim Counselor, CPCU, at 928-6868 . . . and that's it baby . . . no sweat." The member of the Board wonders if Mr. Counselor, a leading insurance broker and a part-time teacher of CPCU classes, has allowed his advertising agency to commercialize the CPCU designation in an undignified and unprofessional manner. Specifically, does the ad copy violate the *G8.1 Guidelines*, which have been incorporated by reference into *Rule R8.1* of the *Code of Professional Ethics?*

OPINION HCS-121

In this case, mindful of the *G8.1* criterion of dignity, the Board feels the ad copy pushes the upper limits of the boundary between good and bad taste. Although standards and values do vary, the Board would be remiss in its duty if it totally acquiesced to the imagination of an advertising agency that, in the eyes of many, compromises the dignity of the CPCU designation. The Board's action would thus be to request Mr. Counselor to cease and desist, and a copy of the *G8.1 Guidelines* would be forwarded to him with an extra copy for the advertising agency.

CASE HCS-122

CPCU Agent is a member of the Board of Directors for the local Boys and Girls Club. He also is called upon for his expertise in regard to coverage for the Club. CPCU Agent designs the coverage for the Club (with other board members' assistance) and places the coverage with one of the carriers he represents. The Boys and Girls Club is appreciative of his dedicated service and has any other interested agent contact CPCU Agent at his/her office for information regarding the bid of the insurance. The Board also instructs other agencies to provide the quotation directly to CPCU Agent, who is to review it in the Committee.

Is there a violation of *Canons 1-9?* Would your opinion change if the CPCU Agent were merely a member of a Club (not in a position of authority)?

OPINION HCS-122

While the hypothetical situation described seems to imply it, it does not specifically state whether or not CPCU Agent has collected his commission on the coverage for the Club that he placed with one of his carriers. It is assumed that this has been the case. With that assumption, the facts clearly represent a situation of a conflict of interest facing CPCU Agent. The essence of such conflict potential lies in the fact that in the circumstances stipulated Agent is in the position to exploit his decision-making position on the Board to his own advantage and to the potential detriment of the Club.

Several provisions of the *Code of Professional Ethics* have a bearing on the subject of the avoidance of conflict of interest that CPCU Agent must keep in mind at all times.

(a) Under *R3.1* and *R3.2* of the Rules of Professional Conduct and *G1.2* of the Guidelines, he must make certain that his acts in designing the coverage for the Club and placing it with one of the carriers he represents do not create even the appearance of impropriety or of allowing the pursuit of personal benefit to interfere with the exercise of sound professional judgment;

(b) *Guideline G3.2* provides that the CPCU should not, to the detriment of the insuring public, engage in any business practice or activity designed to restrict fair competition;

(c) *Guideline G3.3* states that the CPCU should not perform professional services under circumstances that would impair his free and complete exercise of sound professional judgment; and

(d) *Guideline G6.5* requires the CPCU to keep fully informed on legal limitations imposed upon the scope of professional activities.

The foregoing suggests that CPCU Agent, as a director of the Club, must at all times act in such a manner that the Club's interests are preferred over his own. Furthermore, being in the position of at least potentially benefiting from the placement of the coverage at the expense of the Club to which he owes complete loyalty, he must be careful not to violate certain common law and statutory duties pertaining to directors of corporations, thus also becoming guilty of breaching R3.3.

The danger of improper action arising out of the conflict of interest can be easily avoided by CPCU Agent taking the following steps:

1. Fully disclose to the Board of the Club the amount of commission and other compensation he or his firm stands to receive for placing the Club's coverage, and

2. Disqualify himself from voting on or influencing the decision-making process of the Club in any manner that has a bearing on his or his firm's business interest.

By scrupulously adhering to these safeguards, CPCU Agent and all CPCUs in similar positions can continue contributing their expertise as advisors to their organizations and perform significant service to the public.

If the facts are changed so that CPCU Agent is not in a decision-making position for the Club, the key criterion of the conflict of interest, namely the ability to direct business to his own Agency, would not exist. Assuming that ordinary club membership would have no bearing on the placement of the Club's insurance business, then the above-indicated provisions of the *Code* would most likely not apply to CPCU Agent.

The CPCU Society's Code of Ethics

SECTION 3. The Board of Directors, by affirmative vote of two-thirds of its voting members, shall have the authority to expel, suspend, censure, or reprimand any member for conduct in violation of the standards of the Society as set forth in Section 4 of this article, or for conduct in violation of the CPCU professional commitment as adopted and promulgated from time to time by the American Institute for Chartered Property Casualty Underwriters, Inc. The Board of Directors, by affirmative vote of two-thirds of its voting members, shall have the authority to remove any of the board members listed in Article III, Section 2 upon recommendation by the Executive Committee.

SECTION 4. It may be a basis for disciplinary action to commit any of the following acts:

a. Specified Unethical Practices.

(1) To violate any law or regulation duly enacted by any governmental body whose authority has been established by law.

(2) To willfully misrepresent or conceal a material fact in insurance and risk management business dealings in violation of a duty or obligation.

(3) To breach the confidential relationship that a member has with his client or with his principal.

(4) To willfully misrepresent the nature or significance of the CPCU designation.

(5) To write, speak, or act in such a way as to lead another to reasonably believe that the member is officially representing the Society or a chapter of the Society unless the member has been duly authorized to do so.

(6) To aid and abet in the performance of any unethical practice proscribed under this Section.

(7) To engage in conduct which has been the subject of a presidential or Board of Directors directive to cease and desist.

b. Unspecified Unethical Practices.

    (1) A member shall not engage in practices which tend to discredit the Society or the business of insurance and risk management.

    (2) A member shall not fail to use due diligence to ascertain the needs of his or her client or principal and shall not undertake any assignment if it is apparent that it cannot be performed by him or her in a proper and professional manner.

    (3) A member shall not fail to use his or her full knowledge and ability to perform his or her duties to his or her client or principal.

c. Procedure.

    (1) Inquiry.

        (a) Upon written, signed request, the president shall cause an inquiry to be made for the purpose of determining whether there is reasonable basis to believe a violation of this Section has taken place. Requests should be directed to the executive vice president at the national headquarters.

        (b) Inquiry shall be made by a committee appointed by the president. A committee of inquiry (thereafter the "committee") shall be comprised of at least three persons, each of whom shall be a member of the Society. A finding concurred in by the majority of the committees shall be the finding of the committee.

        (c) The committee shall review the written request. If the committee finds that the written request does not state allegations which, if sustained, would constitute a violation of this Section, it shall so notify the president who shall notify the originator of the request. If the committee finds that the written request does state allegations which, if sustained, would constitute a violation of this Section, it shall make inquiries of the member whose conduct is the subject of the request, and may make inquiries of other persons who may have knowledge of pertinent facts and circumstances.

        (d) On the basis of these inquiries, the committee shall find whether there is or is not sufficient evidence to support the allegations in the request, and shall so notify the president who shall notify the member whose conduct is the subject of the request, and the originator of the request.

        (e) The committee may request guidance and advice from the Board of Directors or from the Ethics Committee. Such opinion or advice shall be reduced to writing and appended to the findings of the committee.

(2) Conference.

(a) Within 30 days after receipt of a committee finding that a violation may have occurred, the president shall appoint a conference panel (hereafter the "panel") which shall determine whether the conduct described in the request constitutes unethical conduct. The panel shall be comprised of three members of the Society, at least one of whom shall be a member or past member of the Board of Directors and none of whom shall have served on the committee.

(b) Within 10 working days after appointment, the panel shall send notice of the purported violation by certified mail, return receipt requested, to the last known address of the member whose conduct is the subject of the request.

(c) The notice shall specify the conduct which is the subject of the request and the specified unethical practice involved and/or that the conduct appears to constitute unspecified unethical conduct, and shall set a time and place for a conference which time shall be not less than 30 nor more than 90 days from the date of notice and which place shall be not more than 100 miles from the residence of the member whose conduct is the subject of the request.

(d) At the time and place fixed for the conference, the member whose conduct is the subject of the request shall have an opportunity to be heard, to present witnesses, to question witnesses, and to present written evidence.

(e) Within 10 working days after conclusion of the conference, the panel shall issue its finding. The finding of the panel shall be based exclusively on matters presented at the conference. A finding that the conduct is unethical must be a unanimous finding of the panel and shall be in writing.

(f) The panel finding shall be immediately communicated to the president, to the member whose conduct is the subject of the request, and to the originator of the request. In the case of a finding of specified unethical conduct, the panel shall submit its recommendation for action by the Board of Directors through the president.

(3) Action.

(a) The president shall immediately review the finding of the panel and, in the case of a finding of unspecified unethical conduct, shall direct the member to cease and desist from the unethical conduct. In the case of specified unethical conduct, the Board of Directors shall consider the gravity of the offense and shall expel, suspend, censure, or reprimand the member, and shall direct the member to cease and desist from the unethical conduct. The action of the Board of Directors shall immediately be communicated to the member by certified mail, return receipt requested, at his or her residence.

(b) Expulsion, suspension, or censure of a member shall be reported in CPCU News. Reprimand of a member shall not be reported, and shall be communicated only to the member whose conduct has been found to be unethical.

(c) The Board of Directors shall have prepared a synopsis of each case, without names, resulting in disciplinary action, and shall publish these synopses in CPCU News for the education and guidance of all members.

Glossary

Advisory Opinion An interpretation of the Code of Professional Ethics provided by the Board of Ethical Inquiry. Advisory opinions may take two forms—unpublished and published. Unpublished advisory opinions are informal and intended solely for the guidance of the individuals to whom they are issued. Published advisory opinions are formal, intended for the guidance of all persons subject to the Code.

Altruism (1) Unselfish concern for the welfare of others; selflessness. (2) In ethics, the doctrine that the general welfare of society is the proper goal of an individual's actions: opposed to egoism.

Applicant A CPCU student who has applied to become a CPCU candidate by submitting a matriculation form that has not yet been approved.

Board of Ethical Inquiry (BEI) An eight-member board, chaired by the Ethics Counsel, responsible for implementing established and approved ethics policy.

Candidate A CPCU student whose matriculation application has been approved.

Canons Broad aspirational concepts.

Continuing Professional Development (CPD) Program A recognition program, jointly sponsored by the American Institute and the CPCU Society, which recognizes those who have met specific criteria. The requirements of the CPD program, which are revised from time to time, are automatically distributed to CPCUs who are members of the CPCU Society and are available to others on request.

CPCU (person) A person currently holding the CPCU designation. If the designation is revoked or suspended, that person is no longer a CPCU and is no longer permitted to use the CPCU designation or to display the CPCU key.

CPCU designation The title Chartered Property Casualty Underwriter and/or the abbreviation "CPCU."

CPCU key

Designee   A person who has earned the CPCU designation, whether or not he or she has officially become a CPCU. Those who have met all requirements but are waiting for the date on which they become CPCUs are referred to as designees; those currently receiving the CPCU designation are also considered designees.

Guidelines   Enforceable where they are specifically mentioned in a Rule and therefore become part of that Rule. Other Guidelines are provided to help candidates and CPCUs interpret other Code provisions.

Hypothetical Case Studies   A series of advisory opinions developed when the Code was originally published, and subsequently updated, to illustrate how the Code would be applied to practical situations.

Integrity   Being complete, unbroken, whole, intact, unimpaired, in perfect condition, sound. The quality or state of being of sound moral principle; uprightness, honesty, and sincerity.

Matriculation, Matriculation Process   The process of enrolling as a CPCU student.

New Designee   Jargon used among CPCUs to refer to those just receiving the CPCU designation. New CPCUs are commonly referred to as new designees for their first year until another group of current graduates become new designees.

Nolo Contendere   Latin phrase meaning "I do not wish to argue." In legal proceedings, a plea by which a defendant does not admit guilt but also does not make a defense.

Rules   Specific, enforceable standards that prescribe the minimum levels of required professional conduct. They are enforceable because sanctions may be imposed upon any CPCU or candidate found guilty of a Rules violation.

Suggested Answers to Review Questions

Questions under Canon 1

1. Altruism is unselfish concern for the welfare of others.
2. Professionalism involves serving the public interest.
3. CPCUs should place others' interests above their own by doing their utmost to live up to the high aspirational standards expressed in the Canons.

Questions under Canon 2

1. Any person claiming abilities he or she does not possess misrepresents himself or herself to the people with whom he or she deals.
2. To remain a professional.
3. Remaining informed on technical matters that are essential to maintain competence in my particular position in insurance or risk management.
4. Taking or teaching CPCU and IIA courses or other insurance/risk management courses, teaching similar courses, writing articles, conducting research, and other similar activities.

Questions under Canon 3

1. In addition to obeying laws and regulations, CPCUs should not cause unjust harm to others.
2. Yes. Any CPCU convicted of a felony is subject to automatic suspension of his or her CPCU designation.
3. Under all circumstances, since CPCUs are responsible for knowing the laws and regulations to which they are subject.

Question under Canon 4

CPCUs can often do things that improve insurance contracts, maintain insurers' financial strength, help ensure insurance availability, and help reduce the cost of insurance. CPCUs can also encourage loss control and can support sound research that will lead to improvement in the insurance system.

Question under Canon 5

Yes. A CPCU should assist regulatory authorities investigating any insurance practitioner, including but not limited to CPCUs.

Questions under Canon 6

1. Anyone who is dignified and honorable does not exceed his or her legal limitations, disclose confidential information inappropriately, or misrepresent his or her professional abilities.

2. A CPCU can compensate for his or her own limitations by acknowledging them and drawing on the knowledge of other professionals when necessary. It helps to have established a dignified and honorable relationship with other professionals.

3. In the case of civil or criminal actions, a CPCU should not release confidential information to others unless it is required by law or required by someone to perform legitimate occupational duties.

Questions under Canon 7

1. The Code neither requires nor prohibits lobbying activities. Such activities can be appropriate and desirable in improving the public understanding of insurance and risk management, as well as leading to improvement in the insurance mechanism.

2. CPCUs who lobby or otherwise take a public position on controversial issues should make it clear that they are acting as individuals and not on behalf of the American Institute or the CPCU Society.

Questions under Canon 8

1. A CPCU who is not careful might leave the impression that, because he or she is a CPCU, he or she is acting as a representative of the American Institute for CPCU.

2. By ensuring appropriate and dignified use of the designation and the key.

3. (a) Undignified commercialization and unfair comparisons, as well as any other unethical practices.

(b) On business cards, stationery, office advertising, signed articles, business and professional listings, telephone listings, and in any other manner approved by the American Institute for CPCU.

(c) The CPCU designation should be treated as a personal designation that is associated with the individual CPCU. It should not be used as part of a firm, partnership, or corporate name, trademark, or logo. It should not be affixed to any object, product, or property without permission from the American Institute. The letters "cpcu" should not appear on a vanity license plate, Web page address, e-mail address, or a telephone "number" that is spelled out in letters.

4. The news release available from the American Institute, articles in an employer's publications, and dignified advertisements.

Questions under Canon 9

1. Except for unauthorized use of the CPCU designation, CPCUs are never required to report violations of the Code by CPCUs or CPCU candidates. However, they are ethically required to furnish information to the Ethics Counsel or other appropriate authority investigating a Code violation.

2. Yes, CPCUs are ethically obligated to report the use of the CPCU designation by any non-CPCU—including CPCU candidates.